SHANNON
BETRAYED FROM BIRTH

ROSE MARTIN

SHANNON
BETRAYED FROM BIRTH

THE TRUE STORY OF BRITAIN'S CRUELLEST MOTHER

JOHN BLAKE

www.johnblakepublishing.co.uk

First published in paperback in 2009

ISBN: 978-1-84454-862-0

British Library Cataloguing-in-Publication Data:

A catalogue record for this book is available from the British Library.

Design by www.envydesign.co.uk

Printed and bound by CPI Group (UK) Ltd, Croydon, CR0 4YY

9 10 8

Papers used by John Blake Publishing are natural, recyclable products made from wood grown in sustainable forests. The manufacturing processes conform to the environmental regulations of the country of origin.

CONTENTS

PROLOGUE

'I'm Shannon'

'Stop it, you're frightening me,' the little voice said.

The child's words seemed to be coming from inside a double bed in the middle of the small bedroom, stuffy with the smell of unwashed clothes and stale cigarette smoke. It was the 24th day of the hunt for missing nine-year-old schoolgirl Shannon Matthews, and two CID officers and three of their uniformed colleagues were searching a scruffy council maisonette, one mile from the child's home.

More than 1,800 homes, offices and workshops had been searched since Shannon had seemingly vanished into the bitingly cold air of a February evening in Dewsbury, West Yorkshire. Her mother, Karen Matthews, had become a familiar sight on evening news bulletins, her face contorted with grief and voice heavy with sobs as she begged for any information about her little girl.

But now, in this drab magnolia-painted bedroom, could the search really be coming to an end? Two of the young policemen moved to the edge of the bed and slowly lifted it from the floor. It felt heavier than a normal bed and suddenly a mound of children's clothes tipped out of a hole in the middle of its base.

Then, at the other side of the bed, there was a sound of shuffling and movement. The officers looked across and there, squeezing herself through a hole no larger than 12 inches by 6 inches, was a dark-haired little girl. Her blue eyes and the slight smattering of freckles across her nose and cheekbones were unmistakable.

Her face was tear-stained and she was pale and trembling as she looked up slowly at the burly policeman towering over her and staring at her in astonishment. PC Peter Greenwood leaned forward and helped the little girl to her feet. And then she uttered the words which answered a thousand prayers from the previous three weeks.

'I'm Shannon,' she said quietly.

It was an extraordinary moment – the conclusion of the biggest hunt in the region since the Yorkshire Ripper case 30 years earlier. More than 300 officers had joined the search at a cost of more than £3.2 million. And now it was over. Or at least the hunt for missing Shannon was over. But during the next weeks and months details of the extraordinary plot to abduct the girl would gradually unfold, followed by the arrest first of her captor Michael Donovan and then, to the horror of the entire nation, her own mother, Karen Matthews.

It was a story which shocked Britain to the core – how could any woman allow her own child to be kidnapped and then make repeated television and newspaper appeals for her release, while knowing where she was the entire time? But it was also a story of the remarkable community effort made by the people of Dewsbury Moor to do everything in their power to bring Shannon home.

The terrible case shone a light on life in parts of the country which previously had gone unnoticed by millions and it became regarded as a shocking illustration of 'Broken Britain'. More than anything, it was the story of a quiet little girl who loved collecting Bratz dolls and playing computer games, but who was bitterly betrayed by the woman who, above all, should have been her protector.

It was the story of Shannon, betrayed from birth.

1

KAREN, MOTHER OF SELFISHNESS

It was a bright morning in early September when Karen Matthews stepped out of hospital holding her newborn baby, Shannon. Children across her home town of Dewsbury had just returned to school after the long summer break, kitted out in new uniforms and box-fresh PE kits, for a new year of challenges and opportunities.

But for hours-old Shannon there were to be few such challenges and opportunities in store while she remained with her mum. The baby lying wrapped in a blanket was bonny, with dimples and a healthy cry, but the novelty of bearing her first daughter was already wearing thin on the 23-year-old mother.

Shannon was Karen's third baby – the product of a two-year relationship with 20-year-old local lad Leon Rose. At first, Karen, then a single mum to a toddler, hadn't been able to get enough of Leon who despite still being a teenager was thick-set and seemed manly. Within months, she had become pregnant by him and given birth to her second child, a boy.

The demands of two young children put pressure on the couple, and the relationship became fraught, but, when the new baby was less than six months old, Karen announced she was pregnant again – this time with Shannon. Karen even called Shannon and her elder brother 'twins' because they were both Leon's and were so close in age.

Karen and Leon's relationship lurched along during and after the pregnancy, a rollercoaster of screaming matches and violent rows followed by periods of making-up and relative calm. Little Shannon was barely two when the shouting matches became too much and Leon left for good.

At just 25, Karen's life had already fallen into a depressing cycle of new relationship, pregnancy, birth, break-up, then back to the beginning again. And by the time she hit 32, when Shannon went missing, she had given birth to seven children by six different men. Shannon and her 'twin' were her only kids to share the same father.

During the search for her daughter and her repeated television appeals, Karen Matthews appeared a brutish-looking woman with desperately pale freckled skin, dark rings around her eyes, large, fleshy features and a bushy mass of gingery, auburn hair yanked back into a ponytail with just a few strands of outgrown fringe stuck to her forehead.

But as a child she had been pretty and popular with other kids living nearby. Karen was herself one of seven children – born in 1975 to June and Gordon. Unlike their daughter's future relationships, June and Gordon's marriage weathered the storms of family life and remained strong. They were stalwart examples of Dewsbury's traditional working class.

Gordon worked at Fox's Biscuit Factory – one of the few

remaining big employers in the town. June held down a job in textiles while still working long and hard around the home, cooking fresh food for her kids and trying to ensure they left for school in clean clothes and with scrubbed faces.

Life was generally happy but tough in the Matthews household – it was a constant struggle to make ends meet and the kids were kept strictly in line by their parents. There was little emphasis on education and Karen grew up with few aspirations, her goal in life from an early age being purely to have children. She frequently bunked off school and by the age of 16, with an appalling attendance record, she was still barely able to read. Her IQ, at about 74, was defined as 'borderline low intelligence'.

Karen had rarely left Dewsbury since she was a child and the boundaries of the former mill town were pretty much the perimeters of her existence. Growing up with five brothers, Karen quickly learned that to make herself heard in such a boisterous environment she had to shout loudest and use all her feminine wiles to gain attention.

Her only sister, Julie Poskitt, who is five years older, recalled a largely happy childhood. But she has said it was clear from a very young age that she and Karen were very different. While Julie yearned to grow up and settle down with a steady bloke, Karen was always looking for the next boyfriend, the next compliment and the next bit of excitement. And so it was as a teenager that Karen's life started to slide off the rails.

At 14, Karen's relationship with her mother broke down completely following a series of rows. 'I ended up in a children's home because I couldn't cope with all the stress and lies and stuff,' Karen told a TV documentary team during the search for Shannon. She didn't explain what she meant by 'stress and lies', but the problems were sufficiently bad that she stayed away from home for a couple of years. 'After I got over that they took me out of the children's home,' she said. 'I stayed with them for a bit and then I went to live with my boyfriend's mum. I was about 17 or 18.'

What caused Karen's teenage upheaval and the ensuing chaotic relationships of her twenties and thirties is hard to fathom. Certainly, it is in marked contrast to her sister Julie's long-term marriage to husband John, 40, with whom she had all six of her children.

After her arrest, Karen claimed she was sexually abused at the age of seven. If true, it could be a possible cause of her constant flitting from one relationship to the next, always searching for something new. But other family members have cast doubt on Karen's claim, believing it to be just another of her stories concocted to excuse her behaviour.

Her cousin, Susan Howgate, said she had never heard any stories of abuse. 'I don't know why she had so many partners,' said Susan. 'Maybe she just didn't find the right person.'

When questioned about her string of failed relationships during her trial, Karen spoke self-pityingly about how men 'keep leaving me', but her explanation made little mention of the endless stories of screaming matches and unreasonable behaviour which former partners queued up to relate.

After she turned 16, Karen found part-time work as a cleaner, which, along with benefits, helped to fuel her already extensive smoking and drinking habits. But what she lacked in intelligence and work ethic she certainly made up for in noise and bullishness. She had a vicious temper and when she moved in with her first serious boyfriend, John Bretton, a kitchen assistant, neighbours recalled her screaming and swearing at him day and night.

The couple had met when Karen was living with an uncle of John's. He remembers her then, at 19, as being pretty and nicely turned out. 'It was obvious Karen fancied me and after a few weeks she took me to bed and that was it,' recalled John. 'We never went out anywhere or anything like that, we just met up at the house. She never bothered with the Pill or any other contraception and after a few months she was pregnant.'

John was just 16 and Karen 20 when she gave birth to their son the following year. But what should have been a period of bonding and love for a woman and her first-born child were very different for Karen Matthews. John remembers that her love of cigarettes came before her baby, when they didn't even have enough money to buy milk powder for his bottles.

'I'd taken our stereo into the pawn shop to sell it so we could buy essentials for the baby, nappies and milk,' says John, now 30. 'But typically Karen just wanted cash for cigarettes. She demanded that I go in and get £15 for it. But when I came out with just a tenner she absolutely hit the roof.

'She was stood there screaming and bawling how she needed the extra fiver for smokes. Then she just turned her back and disappeared. I didn't hear from her for two days.' John was left standing in the street with the two-week-old baby, the child's mother apparently totally unconcerned about him. The pair later patched things up and for a short while it was all passion and excitement again.

They moved in together in a council house in

Dewsbury but it was never what most people would call 'home'. Dirty washing was sprawled across the carpets, filthy pots were piled high in the sink and the bathroom was caked in dirt. Teenage John expected Karen to do her share with the chores, particularly as she was no longer working. But his lover had no interest in looking after a home – or even a baby. Instead, she spent the day lying on their tatty sofa watching daytime TV, smoking up to 60 cigarettes a day and chatting to mates over mugs of tea and chocolate biscuits.

With the house in chaos and their newborn baby apparently receiving little attention from his mother, rows between Karen and John became increasingly frequent and worryingly violent. Karen's temper could become explosive at a moment's notice. Alcohol usually played a part in the couple's rows and John complained about being attacked by Karen with saucepans, which although rarely used in the kitchen were always to hand when her drink-fuelled arguments boiled over.

'She had violent rages,' recalled John. 'I was hit by almost everything in the house – pots, pans, even chairs.'

Karen would scream obscenities at John breathlessly for hours, apparently unconcerned that neighbours could hear every word of her ranting. Then one evening John said he returned home to find a strange man there. 'It's over between us,' she told him. 'I've got someone new, so get lost.' And that was the end of Karen Matthews's relationship with the father of her first-born child.

John seemed almost calmly fatalistic about Karen's attitude to relationships. 'Karen just goes from one bloke to the next,' he said. 'She uses them to have a kid, grabs all the child benefit and moves on. I was her first victim.'

It was just a matter of months before Karen had picked up with 'victim' number two – Leon Rose, with whom she went on to have her second son and then Shannon.

Throughout her pregnancies, she had carried on smoking and drank heavily, with little thought of the potential risk to her unborn child. After Karen and Leon split, the boy 'twin' went to live with his dad ten miles away in Huddersfield while toddler Shannon stayed with her mum.

Karen apparently spent little time dwelling on the failed relationship though, and had soon fallen into the arms – and bed – of Paul Hooker, 32. Within months she was pregnant again and gave birth to another little boy – her fourth child. The couple had an on/off relationship for almost three years but again it careered between violent rows, long absences and brief periods of calm.

'In the end he had to move away because she pestered him so much,' recalled a friend, who believes Paul may have been the real love of Karen's life. 'They were going to get married but he backed out because of rumours she was cheating on him. Then she used to go to phone boxes and stalk him by phone. She put him through hell.'

Finally, Paul moved to Cambridgeshire, taking their toddler son with him.

'The day I left Karen she screamed at me to take my son with me. She doesn't care about her kids – she's more interested in men,' Paul said.

By 2000, Karen was on to a new man – unemployed William Marshall, 37 – and baby number five, another little girl, soon followed. But, when that relationship hit the rocks, Karen once again lost any interest in their child. 'Before I took her in, the neighbours used to look after our daughter,' recalled William.

'I was forced to go round there every day to change her nappy and give her her bottle. Karen knew I was only visiting to see my daughter and she wanted more. She said to me one day, "If you don't want to make a go of it, you'd better take your daughter with you when you leave or I'll throw her out on the doorstep." I took her with me that day.'

William now lives with the little girl, a new partner and two new children of their own.

With another child out of the picture, Karen went on to have baby number six, a boy, in January 2003. No father was named on his birth certificate. Despite the physical and emotional rigours of childbirth, and coping with so many needy young children, it seemed Karen Matthews had an insatiable sexual appetite. Perhaps she was simply prepared to do whatever men wanted in a bid to retain their affections, her complicated love life hiding deep-rooted insecurities. But her lovers speak largely of a woman confident about sex when relationships were going well, and threatening and aggressive when they weren't.

One former lover, 67-year-old father-of-six Eddie Clayton, said he was initially flattered by the attentions of a much younger woman. When the couple first had sex – on a sofa in her lounge – she told him not to bother taking his shoes off. Some men might have been put off, but three-times-divorced Eddie said, 'She made me feel young again.'

So smitten was he that he splashed out on a £36.99 engagement ring for her from Argos. But, when Karen's demands in the bedroom proved too much for Eddie's asthma and angina, he had to ask her to calm things down. Their fling finished after three months when Karen secretly started seeing another of her ex-boyfriends, but by then a spotty 18-year-old who used to regularly hang around at the end of Moorside Road had also come to her attention.

'Y'alright?' Karen would shout across at the surly youth as she returned from the corner shop, lugging her carrier bag full of cans of lager and bags of crisps. With his bottle-top glasses, puffy, flat features and teenage spot outbreaks, he was clearly no George Clooney, but Karen had identified her next target – Craig Meehan.

Craig was a full ten years younger than Karen but the age gap didn't bother her. And Karen's complicated domestic set-up – she was by then a mum of six – was apparently no turn-off for him either. Within weeks of their first kiss, Craig had moved into Karen's council house and became the next 'surrogate dad' to the three kids still living with her. Fortunately, Craig was used to large, complicated families himself.

He grew up locally, and his mother, Alice, now lived just a stone's throw from Moorside Road. One of nine children herself, Alice was unhappy about Craig's relationship with Karen though, thinking her precious son could have done better for himself. Craig's sister, Amanda, lived next door to him and Karen, with her bus driver husband Neil and their three children, while his other sister, Caroline, also lived close by.

Karen, Craig, Amanda and Neil were close mates and always in and out of each other's houses, and the kids would play for hours on the adjacent playing field. Soon after getting together with Craig, Karen announced pregnancy number seven and went on to give birth to another little girl. Everyone locally – including Craig – appeared to assume it was his child. It was only when DNA tests were taken during Shannon's disappearance that it emerged the little girl wasn't his at all. Her father remains unknown.

For four years before Shannon's abduction, Karen's life with Craig and the kids appeared at first glance to be reasonably settled. But, despite having remained under the same roof for so long, there were big problems in their relationship, as was about to become clear. The kids were used to regular screaming matches and door-slamming as Craig stormed out for the umpteenth time.

For Karen, it was history repeating itself yet again. Another relationship, another kid (even if the child wasn't really Craig's) and now another break-up around the corner. What effect all this upset might have had on her children seemed barely to nudge Karen's consciousness, or conscience. She wasn't happy and wanted a way out – and, for Karen, what she wanted was what happened.

She was a woman whose actions had been ruled by selfishness and desire for so long that her children's needs came such a long way down her list of priorities they barely registered at all.

2

SHANNON – BORN TO BE FORGOTTEN

Before Shannon Matthews could even walk or talk, she had been betrayed by the person who should have been her constant protector, her mother Karen. Even in the first few weeks after birth, when most mothers can barely stop themselves from breathing in that smell of newness, from touching that silkiest skin and counting the tiny toes and fingers, Karen had little interest in her child.

With her relationship with Shannon's father, Leon, in its death throes, and finding herself struggling to cope with the needs of a baby and two toddlers, Karen moved back in with her parents. She had got over her differences with her mum, June, who was determined to support her grandchildren in any way that she could.

'Shannon was brought from the hospital by a nurse to stay in my care,' recalled June, 66. 'Karen came from the hospital to stay here too for about two months, then she took the children home with her. I brought Shannon up for the first two months.'

But when Karen and her children finally moved back into their own council house, away from June and Gordon's watchful gaze, things quickly spiralled out of control.

The worried grandparents tried to keep an eye on what Karen was doing with her kids by visiting regularly, but their trips just made them increasingly concerned at the goings-on. 'Once I found Shannon, covered in sick and with a dirty nappy in the corner of the room,' recalled June. 'She smelled awful and was really wailing. I screamed at Karen to change and bathe her, but I ended up doing it myself.'

And Shannon wasn't the only one of Karen's children who was a victim of their mother's neglect. 'I once walked into the house and found one of the little ones wrapped up in a dirty curtain on the stairs, looking like a mummy, and crying and wailing,' said June. 'Karen had just left the poor thing there, as if it was a normal thing to do.'

On another occasion, June turned up at the house unexpectedly to discover Shannon eating bread off the floor, while Karen and some friends tucked into pie and chips. 'Karen and her mates were sat around on the sofas laughing and joking,' she said. 'They all had huge plates of steak and kidney pie, chips and peas. But poor Shannon was sat on the floor. She was dirty faced and was eating dry bread straight off the carpet. It was despicable. She looked awful – it was as if they didn't even know she was there.'

Shannon was once again invisible to her mother, and even her grandmother's attempts to get her noticed fell on deaf ears. 'I confronted Karen and asked why Shannon wasn't having the same as them,' said June. 'She just looked at me and said, "She likes what she's got."'

Several of Karen's children went to live with Gordon and June for periods of time when it became clear she was totally unable to cope or had given up interest. For the children, these were respite periods of happiness. But once they returned home the neglect resumed. If Karen had been suffering from post-natal depression or an illness, there might have been greater sympathy from her family and friends. But it was simply her preference to spend her time – and money – on boozing, smoking and watching daytime TV that angered and frustrated those around her.

Her children were largely an inconvenience and, having packed three of them off to live with their fathers and keeping four at home herself, it seemed she often lost track of how many she actually had. In the early days after Shannon was abducted, it was widely reported she had six children – because Karen herself had forgotten to mention one of them.

Karen never cooked proper meals for her kids, preferring to heat frozen chips and nuggets or handing them takeaways still in the wrappers. The house was so dirty that at times it became a health hazard, infested with mice and beetles feasting on the empty pizza boxes and Styrofoam takeaway cartons which spilled out of a rarely emptied bin and on to the kitchen floor.

Karen's sister Julie, 38, a senior care worker at a nursing home, was shocked and appalled by her sister's poor quality of parenting. 'I remember she came round ours once and one of her babies had a plastic bag taped to its bum instead of a nappy,' she said.

Julie and her husband, John, gave Karen money to go and buy nappies but she came back without them.

'We later found out she'd spent the money on a pack of

cigs and some cheap cider. That happened a lot,' said Julie, who lived three miles away from Karen in Thornhill, on the south side of Dewsbury. 'She'd have money – either in benefits or from friends or family, but it would never go on her kids. She would spend it on stuff like crisps, sweets and pop.'

On other occasions, Karen saved on the cost of nappies by using old towels taped to the children's bottoms.

The sisters had been estranged since before Shannon's disappearance and it is clear there is deep resentment between them. 'She just never settled down like I did,' Julie said. 'Even when she had kids, her love life just continued as usual. Right from the time she had her first baby, I knew she was never going to make a good mother. It was just not going to happen. I have seen her hit her kids. And not just once or twice. It happened again and again. It was truly awful.'

Julie told how her sister could not even be bothered to hold bottles to feed her babies, preferring instead to prop them up with a cushion, even when the tots were just weeks old. 'I was disgusted,' said Julie. 'I mean, what kind of mother would do that? The house was absolutely filthy. There would always be food all over the floor in her kitchen. It was a real state and certainly no place for children.

'Once we were round at her house and her son was crying. But instead of hugging him or kissing him, she threw him up in the air and he landed on the couch. We were shocked. My mum was furious. But Karen just laughed and said, "Well, it's a mangy little bastard."'

Karen's children quickly became used to the succession of men who traipsed in and out of their lives. They were always instructed by their mother to call her boyfriends 'Dad' – no matter how short-lived the relationship was. 'The poor things didn't know what they were up to,' said Julie.

In her need to get money for food, fags and alcohol, Karen even took to stealing items donated to charity shops – dragging her children with her. 'She'd take Shannon in her pram and hover outside the British Heart Foundation and Help the Aged before they were open,' said Julie. 'People used to drop bags of stuff outside the shops before they went to work. And Karen would be there, waiting. Once they'd left, she would put the bags in the pram, and shoot off. I used to see her flogging the stuff at a car boot sale the following Sunday.'

Karen's total lack of compassion was brutally brought home, though, when she didn't even attend the funeral of Julie's two-year-old son, Jonathan, who had been born with Down's Syndrome. She had also snubbed the little boy's christening. 'Everyone else was there but not Karen,' recalled Julie. 'There was no excuse, no card, no flowers.'

Many friends, relatives and former lovers were convinced Karen's increasing brood was just a means of ensuring greater social security benefits. Whatever the reasoning, though, it was soon apparent that her lack of parenting skills, combined with laziness and selfishness, meant she was simply not capable of caring for the children she already had – let alone those she was to go on to have.

Julie became so concerned she phoned Social Services. 'She showed no love and it was heartbreaking,' said Julie. 'I contacted Social Services three times but when they went to her house they said they didn't see any signs of neglect. But her house was absolutely filthy.'

And Julie was not the only one concerned about the conditions Shannon and her siblings had to endure.

Neighbour Claire Wilson, 33, also telephoned the local Social Services department after hearing Shannon and her brothers and sisters sobbing through the walls of their home. Meanwhile, Karen would be holding all-night parties for local lads downstairs, either unaware of or unconcerned by her children's distress.

'The warning signs that Shannon needed help were there six years before she disappeared,' said Claire. 'Social Services failed her. She needed help. I know I wasn't the only one that was telling them. I know the school knew because I even contacted the education authority because I was running out of places to ring up and say, "Look, something's going on."

'Lads used to lean out of the window, drinking, smoking and swearing. You could hear Shannon crying. The stereo was blaring 24 hours a day and you could hear crying on top of that. Dirt was caked on the soles of her feet like cement. I once rolled the dirt off her feet. It was like glue, really stuck on. She'd always flinch back from you if you were trying to get a smile out of her.'

Shannon was just four when the family moved into their three-bed council house, three-quarters of the way down Moorside Road in Dewsbury Moor. The following year, she started at the local infants school but within weeks she was standing out from the other youngsters in her class. Partly it was because of her shy grin and pretty freckled features, but partly it was because she already bore the hallmarks of neglect. Her hair was often matted and unwashed and her clothes had the stale smell of those that are rarely washed. Teachers added their voices to those of neighbours and family members who had called Social Services to express concerns.

In late 2002/early 2003, Shannon and her siblings were placed on the at-risk register by Kirklees Council, although they still remained with their mum in the family home. Social workers were particularly concerned about reports that the youngsters had been left home alone all night – and that there was serious alcohol abuse going on around them.

An investigation by the BBC's *Panorama* programme following Karen's trial discovered Kirklees Council commissioned a psychological report on Karen around the time her children were placed on the at-risk register. The report called for Karen to be kept under constant supervision, because her 'ability to protect her children is compromised by her inability to successfully place the children's needs above her own'. The report concluded, 'I believe that Karen will require constant monitoring and support throughout the lives of her children.'

Nevertheless, just over a year later in 2004, Karen's children were removed from the at-risk register. It appeared they were no longer thought to be in danger from their mother or anyone else.

Panorama also discovered a 'serious allegation of neglect' just three months later but social workers decided no further action was necessary and that the children weren't at risk of 'significant harm'. The report said the family appeared to be 'settling down' and as a result social workers were keen to reduce their involvement. Occasional visits by members of the Social Services department did continue, but Karen was informed in advance of the visits and had sense enough to ensure the children appeared as though they were being well looked after.

'I always knew when Social Services were due because Karen would ask to borrow money from me,' said her mum. 'When I asked what it was for, she would say, "I have to buy food to fill the cupboards – the social worker is coming." It was the only time she filled the cupboards with proper food.'

Kirklees Council has refused to confirm whether Shannon was ever on the protection register or how many times it was contacted by people concerned about her well-being. However, many relatives and neighbours retained serious concerns about Karen's treatment of her children right up to the point of Shannon's disappearance. But others were quick to defend Karen when allegations about her complicated domestic life emerged in the newspapers.

Close friend Petra Jamieson summed up the feelings of many on the estate who felt themselves under fire from the middle classes pontificating about their family set-ups and way of life. 'Whose family's perfect anyway?' she said. 'I know mine isn't and a lot of other people's isn't. Karen's not the first person in the world to have kids by different blokes – not the first person and she won't be the last person.'

But it wasn't so much the number of children Karen had had by different men, it was the fact that she seemed either unwilling or unable to care for them properly. And, as the Social Services report had recorded years before, she simply was incapable of putting her kids' needs before her own.

When Shannon disappeared, Karen was receiving £350 in benefits – or 'my wage' as she called it. Craig was also bringing home about £300 a week working on the fish counter at Morrisons in Heckmondwike. He claimed all his money went on bills and food for the kids, but in reality a large chunk of their income was going on Karen and Craig's £30-a-day cigarette habit plus the endless bags of lager tins and takeaway food being carried into the home.

Karen had also fallen into debt with loan sharks, and repayments took another sizeable proportion of her cash.

And there is little doubt Craig and Karen preferred spending what money they did have on themselves before considering the children's needs. In the front room of 24 Moorside Road there were two home computers – one for Craig and the other for Karen. Against another wall sat a large television beneath which was a DVD player, a Sky box and an Xbox used by Craig and his mates.

In the period immediately before Shannon's disappearance, there was clearly much unhappiness behind the yellowing net curtain of 24 Moorside Road. To casual observers, it seemed that the balance of power in Karen and Craig's relationship was very much weighted in Karen's direction. She was physically larger than her somewhat gormless-looking partner, whose passions in life appeared to be playing on his Xbox and collecting model cars. Craig looked younger than his age and his mouth invariably hung open, as though in a constant state of confusion. Karen appeared far older and more confident, with a louder voice and a stronger physical presence.

But behind the closed doors of their home the reality of their relationship was more complex. In fact, Craig was the more intelligent and articulate of the pair. And, as the wage-earner, he knew Karen was dependent on his money. But she had become obsessed that he was seeing other women while claiming to be at work.

Craig would return home from a late shift, tired, cold and stinking of fish, only to then face a barrage of screaming and swearing from a half-cut Karen, convinced he'd been out with his 'bit on the side'. Craig always denied cheating on Karen, whom he said he still loved, but admitted he stormed out on many occasions, sick of Karen's outrageous claims.

June and Gordon Matthews, the parents of Karen Matthews, claimed that, at the end of visits to their own house, Shannon and her brothers and sister would often be in tears, desperate not to have to return home. 'It was heartbreaking seeing them like that,' said June. 'It couldn't have been more obvious they didn't want to go back.'

Accusations of violence towards Karen and the children were levelled at Craig Meehan but he has always strenuously denied them. Craig was also defended by Karen's cousin, Susan Howgate. 'I have known Craig for six or seven years and he is the kindest, gentlest person,' she said at the time. 'He loves kids and he would never, ever hurt anyone.'

The house was filthy, with piles of rubbish in every corner, shoes scattered up and down the thinly carpeted staircase and damp clothes attempting to 'air' on a plastic rack in the kitchen which stank of week-old takeaways and the fug of stale cigarette smoke.

The kids' hair went unwashed and their pale faces showed it could have been days since they'd had a decent meal, let alone a vegetable. Karen rarely cooked and the family lived largely on takeaway food from the chip shop down the road or the local pizza delivery service.

Just like at her infants school, teachers at Westmoor Junior School were worried about the state of Shannon and her siblings. On several occasions she arrived for lessons with dirt visibly caked to her neck and arms and her clothes stinking. It later emerged that the headteacher had warned Social Services about their concerns on a number of occasions.

There were also worries about Shannon's levels of concentration. Always a quiet, shy girl, she had become even more subdued and was unable to focus for long periods on reading and writing. But no teacher could possibly have guessed the real reason for the change in Shannon – that her mother had been systematically drugging her with tranquilisers to make her easier to control.

It was only after her release from captivity that a medical examination showed Shannon had been fed drugs for almost two years – back to when she had been just seven – which would have acted as a 'chemical cosh', making her sleep for long periods and act docile when awake. Having a child asleep or utterly compliant would have perfectly suited Karen's desire to live her life unaffected by the needs of her children.

Friends who were unaware of Karen's means of keeping her daughter under control defended her parenting at the time of Shannon's disappearance. Susan Howgate, one of her staunchest supporters, said, 'Karen is a brilliant mum and loves her children 100 per cent.'

Other neighbours told how Shannon had dedicated a school project on the topic of 'Thanks' to Karen. She wrote, 'I love my mum because she does nice things with me.'

But teachers, relatives and social workers were increasingly of the opinion that there were few 'nice things' going on at home for Shannon. Perhaps her project was more an attempt to fit in with the other children in her class, the neatly turned-out kids whose mothers were always waiting at the school gate and who took them home to a clean house and a hot dinner.

For, however much Shannon might have wanted to escape the chaos of Moorside Road, there appeared little chance of it. Up until the previous summer she had enjoyed regular trips to her real dad, Leon Rose, who lived ten miles away in the rural village of Kirkburton, near Huddersfield. But then Leon and Karen fell out over money and Shannon's contact with her dad ground to a halt.

To Shannon, Leon's home had seemed a million miles away from the built-up bleakness of Dewsbury Moor. She loved the open space where she could play for hours with her natural brother, her two new step-siblings and their little dog. She even got on well with her dad's new partner Tracey Matthews – who, although sharing the same surname, was no relation to her.

On their last family outing before relations were severed, Shannon had enjoyed a trip with her dad, brother and step-family to a Thomas the Tank Engine theme day. Karen Matthews wasn't one for family outings, which made the event all the more special for Shannon. The four children all whooped with excitement as the light railway trundled along on the day trip. Even young Shannon must have wondered why her 'normal' life in Dewsbury Moor had to be so very different to this.

The next day, though, she was back to reality with Karen and Craig. And the reality of daily life at Moorside Road was grim. Some family members believe Shannon and her siblings may even have been on the verge of being taken into care when she went missing. Kirklees Council has always refused to comment on this.

By early 2008, Karen could rarely even be bothered to make the kids' breakfast, taking them round to her mum's house instead, where they'd be given toast and a drink.

With the older kids in school, Karen would return home to spend the day slumped on her black, leather-effect sofa, watching daytime TV – including her favourite programme *The Jeremy Kyle Show*, with its constant stream of dysfunctional life stories which so closely mirrored her own.

Looking down on Karen as she sat on the sofa was a large picture on the chimney breast of the four children that still lived with her – including Shannon. But, while most parents might have literally hundreds of photographs of their children, the portrait was one of just a handful that Karen possessed. After Shannon's disappearance, she struggled to find enough good pictures of her daughter for the police to release.

When she wasn't watching television, Karen spent the rest of her days browsing eBay and other internet sites on her computer, while Craig played games on his own machine on the other side of the room. By mid-afternoon, Karen would be into her second packet of fags and drinking cans of lager, unworried by all the dirt and clutter.

And while all around the country other little girls went running home from school, eager to see their mums for a kiss and a cuddle, Shannon would trail reluctantly up the road, always nervous of what might await her next behind the family's yellowing uPVC front door. Back home, she would retreat to her bedroom, away from the inevitable screaming and shouting which marked Craig's return from work.

It was within this chaotic whirlwind of relationships and tensions that family life, such as it was, had been blundering on in the run up to 19 February 2008. Such was the confusion and noise of it all that the shy, timid Shannon had become largely forgotten. She had slipped from baby to toddler to schoolgirl virtually unnoticed by a mother, wholly wrapped up in her own relationship dramas, boozing and partying.

Poor Shannon's life had been shaped by disinterest and neglect from the very beginning. But things were about to become far, far worse when her mother did finally stop to notice her.

3

MISSING

S hannon Matthews woke on the morning of Tuesday, 19 February 2008 and climbed down the ladder at the side of the bunk bed she shared with her two-year-old sister. Daylight was just coming through the tissue-thin, doggy-patterned curtains at her window. Looking around, she would have seen the chaos and grime which had become the norm during her nine years of life so far.

An attempt to brighten up the room by painting one wall sky blue and the other pink had come to a sad end when half the pink wallpaper was ripped away and never replaced. On the blue walls there were pencil and crayon doodlings.

Most poignantly was one message written in felt-tip pen in Shannon's own handwriting: 'I want to live with my Dad'. Shannon dreamed of moving to live with her dad, natural brother and step-family. But it was six months now since she had last seen them and a sense of desertion can only have added to her sadness.

As the elder sister, Shannon had naturally claimed the top bunk in the girls' bedroom and she turned it into a refuge from the confusing and hostile adult world downstairs. Her dolls and teddies were lined up on top of her pink duvet, while on the windowsill sat her prized collection of antique porcelain dolls, and above the wardrobe were the Bratz dolls which she had begged for over the past few birthdays and Christmases.

The royal-blue bedroom carpet was worn and rough; a half-hearted attempt had been made to cover stains with a pair of Panda and Tiger rugs, although they too were now grubby.

It was a bitterly cold morning even inside 24 Moorside Road and Shannon slipped on her 101 Dalmatians dressing gown to protect herself from the chill before clambering over the discarded clothes and toys on her bedroom carpet and out on to the landing.

Shannon spent a lot of time in her room, away from the drunken screaming and shouting that often shaped life between Craig and her mum downstairs. She'd even scrawled in pencil on her bedroom door 'Shannon's room. Keep out' inside a heart shape. The general state of neglect in the house meant it was normal for the kids to draw over doors and walls. After her disappearance, friends and neighbours described Shannon as 'quiet', 'shy' and 'timid'. But they also told how she had enjoyed computer games, painting and playing with her dolls.

On 19 February, Shannon was no doubt particularly quiet after a huge row in the house the previous night. As she wandered silently downstairs, holding on to the slightly sticky handrail and stepping over odd clothes and discarded trainers on the brown stair carpet, she must have wondered what was in store for her that morning.

The previous evening, she had dared to swear at Craig during an argument and then all hell had broken loose and Shannon fled in floods of tears to her uncle Martin's house nearby. 'Shannon came here at teatime,' recalled Martin. 'She said to me, "Please can I stay here tonight? I can't go home as I'm in trouble and I've been grounded." She said she'd had an argument with Craig and had sworn at him.'

He felt uncomfortable in getting involved in the dispute and reluctantly told her she had to go home. He asked his ten-year-old daughter, Tyler, to walk with Shannon who had cried all the way home.

Quite often Shannon would go to her nan, June's, house for breakfast or would grab something to eat at a special school breakfast club. But that morning the atmosphere was still tense at home and Shannon clearly wanted to escape to school just as soon as she could. She slipped into her Westmoor Junior black jumper, white cotton T-shirt and black trousers, then pulled on her puffa jacket coat with the furry hood and wedged her feet into her prized pink Bratz boots with the grey furry edges

Karen was still in a foul mood and, as the previous night's argument resumed, she screamed at her daughter to get out of the house and not come back. As Shannon trudged out of the green front gate just after 8.00am, her mother's scalding words ringing in her ears, she could have had little idea of how true they would turn out to be: from that moment Shannon would never go back to 24 Moorside Road.

On the half-mile walk to school, Shannon saw her cousins – Martin's children – and told them all about her mother's angry outburst. There was little to lift her spirits that chillingly cold morning apart from the thought of her first swimming lessons that afternoon at Dewsbury Sports Centre.

In her bag she had packed a blue striped towel and the pink and black two-piece 'tankini' costume her nan had bought her at a flea market during a trip to Scarborough a couple of years earlier. It was a beautiful colour and Shannon had been looking forward to finally getting the chance to wear it. Karen and Craig had had little interest in teaching Shannon to swim and she was thrilled at the thought of practising her strokes in the water with all her classmates.

Shannon was in Year Four at school and, despite her teachers' concerns about her, she generally received good reports. She wasn't top of the class, but not a troublemaker either. As in most things, that was Shannon's lot – neither one extreme nor the other, the kind of good-natured shy girl who could all too easily get lost in the crowd and slip into obscurity. She was a nice-looking girl – again neither stunning nor unattractive but somewhere in the middle. Her long, dark hair was usually tied up from her face in a scrunchy elastic band and her fringe, slightly lopsided in the last photographs taken before her disappearance, lay heavy on her forehead.

Shannon's 4ft 1ins frame still bore a hint of puppy fat but she was growing up fast – her family life left her with no option. Freckles dusted her nose and face which often looked serious and was more inclined to a shy grin than a broad beaming smile and the worries of her small world could be seen lying behind Shannon's blue eyes.

Experts think it likely that, arriving at class that morning, Shannon would have felt some effects of the drugs her mother had been feeding her over such a long period of time. Maybe she felt confused and slightly fuzzy without understanding why, and it must certainly have been an unpleasant sensation.

In the classroom, Shannon sat in her usual chair next to best friend Megan Aldridge. The pair had stuck to each other like glue for the past two years. They were both shy and felt awkward around some of the other more confident kids but they found comfort in each other's company. Megan remembered Shannon being a little more withdrawn than normal that day, but nothing really out of the ordinary.

As Shannon began her lessons, Karen was at home, sprawled on the sofa to watch television and to browse eBay for bargains. Later in the morning, Craig's cousin Ryan Meehan came round to play computer games and she popped out to her mum's house.

June recalled noticing her daughter had a black eye. 'Karen said she'd had an argument with Craig,' said June. 'It was clear she was upset. She told me she'd had a fall, but I knew there was more to it. She'd been rowing with Craig that morning.'

Meanwhile, after school lunch, Shannon and her classmates boarded a coach to take them to Dewsbury Sports Centre for the eagerly awaited swimming lesson. As usual, Shannon and Megan sat next to each other and Megan again noticed that Shannon was particularly quiet.

'Shannon was quiet on the way to swimming instead of talking all the time like she would normally. I didn't ask her why,' recalled Megan, a delicate-looking girl with long hair and glasses. 'But when we got to the lesson and had two armbands on each arm we started giggling and splashing. It was funny. She was a better swimmer than me.'

After an hour of swimming and splashing, the girls chatted happily in the changing rooms as they changed back into their school uniforms. Shannon and Megan were again side-by-side as they walked from the changing rooms back to the maroon-coloured coach waiting outside to collect the class. Shannon appeared carefree as she swung the plastic bag carrying her damp swimming costume around her wrist on her way out through the sports-centre doors.

Little could she have realised that those moments, at around 3.00 pm, as she stepped through the reception area and out towards the coach would soon be viewed by millions. Because those were Shannon's final movements caught on CCTV before her disappearance and they would be played and replayed countless times on television stations across the country as the hunt to find her became increasingly desperate.

On the bus on the way back to school, Megan recalled, Shannon's mood was low again. 'We got on the bus home and Shannon was really, really quiet. A girl came up to her and started bullying her and I told her to go away or I would tell the teacher, so she walked off.'

Shannon told Megan she was going straight home after getting off the bus. When it pulled up in Church Lane outside Westmoor Junior ten minutes later, Shannon stepped on to the pavement behind Megan. One of the teachers, Mrs Tingle, saw Shannon get off the bus but neither she nor Megan noticed which direction Shannon headed in. The children were all racing to get home out of the cold wind as quickly as possible and in the confusion Shannon set off in a different direction to her usual route. Again the quiet little girl had gone unnoticed by anyone.

MISSING

In the weeks that followed, as her last moves were constantly analysed, it seemed as if seconds after stepping off the bus Shannon had simply disappeared into thin air on that bitter afternoon. No one said goodbye to her. No one saw her go. And for the next 24 days there were no confirmed sightings, abandoned clothes or vaguest clues as to where she might be.

Shannon Matthews was missing.

4

A WICKED PLOT

Karen Matthews slammed the mug of tea down on the café table and plonked herself heavily in the chair. It was a bitterly cold winter morning and the shop's windows were steamed up by shoppers trying to warm themselves away from the biting wind cutting through Dewsbury.

The tiny café opposite the popular Mermaid Fish and Chip Restaurant was hardly the kind of place that it might be imagined one of Britain's most shocking criminal plots would be hatched. But it was here that Karen Matthews began to flesh out the plan that had taken root in her mind – to stage a kidnapping of her nine-year-old daughter Shannon.

Sitting opposite Karen across the smeary Formica table sat 39-year-old Michael Donovan, the man who was to hide Shannon for the 24 long days of her disappearance. Even now detectives are still not entirely clear how much of the plan lay with each of the key players. In court, they each blamed the other for what happened. But it seems most likely that, from that café meeting, Karen was intent on kidnapping her daughter. And most probably it was with the motivation of receiving a £50,000 reward for Shannon's 'discovery'. She desperately needed the cash to pay off the loan sharks on her back but also wanted to enjoy the riches she had previously only been able to dream about.

Of course, there was no guarantee there would even be a reward and even less chance Karen and Michael could have ever got away with claiming it without being rumbled. And how did Karen intend to prevent Shannon from telling people where she had been? But such details weren't bothering Karen.

Karen and Michael had first met in a pub on the Heckmondwike Road in Dewsbury at a wake following the funeral of Craig's dad, Brian Meehan, who had died of a heart attack, aged 60, the previous November. The pair had shared a quiet moment smoking outside the pub.

Then later, when Craig, drowning his grief in endless cans of lager, started rowing and becoming aggressive, Karen had fled to his mother Alice's house. It was there she met Michael again and the pair began chatting. By that point they'd both been drinking for several hours and Karen found Michael – an introverted loner with a very low IQ – a willing shoulder to cry on. As they sat close to each other in Alice Meehan's kitchen, Karen confided how she was thinking of leaving Craig.

One fellow mourner who wandered into the kitchen later claimed Karen was sitting on Michael's knee and they 'were all over each other'. It was then, amid a drunken fumble, that Michael offered Karen his house as a bolt-hole should she need it. In later police interviews, Karen claimed she turned down the offer and that Michael reacted by giving her a look of 'disgust'.

In the weeks that followed, Michael, who lived about a mile from Dewsbury Moor on an estate in Batley Carr, paid regular visits to visit his sister, Alice. She was then staying with her daughter Caroline just yards from Karen and Craig. It is thought Karen and Michael met again during this time, and Craig's sister Amanda has said, looking back, she is convinced they were having a relationship, although both have always denied it.

Then, one morning at the start of 2008, Michael was driving his Peugeot 406 on his way to visit Alice in Dewsbury Moor when he was flagged down by Karen. She was pushing the youngest child's pink buggy along the pavement when she stepped out into the road and hailed him over to the kerb.

Michael wound down the window and Karen glanced up and down the road then leaned inside. 'I've got a problem. I wondered if you can sort it out but I don't want nobody else to know about this,' Karen said, according to Michael's later police interviews.

The pair arranged to meet a couple of days later at the Dewsbury café.

Sitting across the table from each other separated by two mugs of tea, the pair of conspirators must have appeared a very odd-looking couple that morning. Her: thick-set with a brutish loud voice barking orders across the table. Him: bony faced with thin lips and a barely audible tone. In a battered baby buggy at the side of the table sat Shannon's two-year-old sister.

According to Michael, Karen first asked him if he could lend her £20,000, although on another occasion he said that request was made the time she flagged him down. When Michael said there was no way he had that kind of money, she took an intake of breath and revealed her alternative plan 'to get some money'.

Michael claimed first Karen asked him to 'look after' her eldest son. But Michael flatly rejected the plan, saying he didn't know him. Karen paused, then came out with her next suggestion: 'Can you look after Shannon instead?' According to Michael, Karen said there would be a 'bigger reward out of this if she went missing'. After all, Shannon was younger, sweeter and more photogenic than her older brother.

Karen then explained to Michael that he would have to look after Shannon after she reported the child missing. She said once the reward money figure had hit £50,000 she would tell him what to do next. In a moment of high drama, probably unknown in that little Dewsbury café either before or since, Karen then pushed an A4 sheet of paper across the table to Michael detailing his instructions.

The paper listed the date and time he was supposed to wait for Shannon and instructions about what he was to do with her. After learning his instructions by heart, he was told to dispose of the paper 'down the toilet'.

Karen and Michael's accounts of the café meeting differ significantly. Michael later claimed he wanted nothing to do with it, but then Karen turned heavy, threatening to set three lads on him unless he complied with her orders. Michael said he knew the names of the youngsters she mentioned and one of them was believed to have stabbed a man to death. When she told him if he didn't help her he 'would be dead', Michael caved in. He later claimed he never wanted any part of the reward money.

Karen later refuted Michael's story that it was all her plan – and to this day portrays *herself* as an innocent victim in the kidnapping. Certainly, whether she was intellectually capable of concocting such an elaborate plan on her own remains a subject of debate among detectives. Both she and Michael are of pitifully low intelligence and many feel they would have struggled to get away with the scheme for as long as they did alone.

One theory was that they had stolen the whole idea from an episode of the Channel 4 TV drama *Shameless* that had recently aired. The series followed the exploits of the feckless, drunken Gallagher family living on a fictional sink estate in Manchester. Some of the show's characters could have been modelled on Karen Matthews.

Just a month before Shannon's disappearance, one episode of *Shameless* featured a fake kidnap and ransom plot. In the programme, it was announced on local news that lazy dad Frank Gallagher had won £500,000 on the Lottery. His teenage daughter didn't believe it and so staged the kidnapping of her younger brother, issuing a ransom demand to see if her father would pay. But all the time her brother was hidden at a friend's house just a few doors away.

Detectives on the Shannon inquiry later asked for tapes of the programme before questioning Karen Matthews. Clearly, Karen watched dozens of hours of television every week but no one has ever been able to prove she was a fan of that particular drama. What was not in doubt is that over the previous nine months she had been following the huge media coverage of the ongoing search for missing Madeleine McCann.

The search for Madeleine, snatched weeks before her fourth birthday while on holiday in the Algarve in Portugal, had led to a worldwide hunt and huge amounts of money donated to the 'Find Madeleine' campaign. The thought of such riches being up for grabs seems the most likely factor to have shaped Karen's thinking at the start of that year.

But whatever the motives behind the horrific scheme plotted at the meeting at the Dewsbury café, the wheels for its execution were already in motion. Shy, timid Shannon had been selected, like a sacrificial lamb for slaughter, as the means to bring her mother the cash she so desperately wanted.

5

THE HUNT BEGINS

Detectives often speak about the 'Golden Hours' in missing-persons investigations – that critical time immediately after disappearance when they can gather the clues and information that ultimately determine whether they solve a case or not.

For locals on the Dewsbury Moor estate that bitterly cold night that Shannon disappeared, every moment of those Golden Hours was spent searching sheds, bins and outhouses in the hope of finding her or some clue as to her whereabouts. All around the estate cries of 'Shannon, Shannon' could be heard being called out into the damp air.

But the Golden Hours for Karen Matthews that Tuesday evening were very different. Shannon was due home at around 3.30pm. When she didn't appear, Karen was supposedly racked with worry, but in reality she went shopping with Craig's sister Amanda Hyett to help her buy a sat-nav GPS device for husband Neil. Then, after calling 999, she popped off supermarket shopping, again with

Amanda. She returned home later, tossing a crate of lager on the sofa, apparently unconcerned the rest of Dewsbury Moor was out in force looking for her daughter.

In between her shopping jaunts, Karen first raised the alarm at around 4.00pm when she knocked on the door of neighbour Victoria Saunders, saying she was concerned Shannon hadn't returned from school. Shannon was usually one of the first kids back to Moorside Road after the final bell rang at Westmoor Junior. Ten minutes later, she called the school office, asking if the bus had returned from the swimming trip.

Then, at ten to seven in the evening – just as the adverts were starting before *Emmerdale* on TV – Karen made the 999 call which set into motion what was to become a mammoth multimillion-pound investigation and one of Britain's biggest-ever missing-person inquiries.

If Karen had any awareness of the drama she was about to unleash as she punched the three nines into her phone, she would have been quaking. But her voice in the message recorded by the emergency services which is transcribed below, revealed someone extremely comfortable with their lies:

Operator: Police emergency.
Karen: Hiya, I want to report me daughter as missing please.
Operator: Right, how old is she?
Karen: Nine.
Operator: Nine?
Karen: Yeh.
Operator: When did you last see her?
Karen: She went to school this morning.

Operator: Right, has there been any arguments or anything like that?

Karen: No none at all.

Operator: Have you been in touch with her friends or anybody like that?

Karen: I've been everywhere I can think of, friends, family and everywhere I can think of.

Operator: And nobody at all can give you any information of where she can be?

Karen: No.

Operator: Does she go to school and come back on her own normally then?

Karen: Yeh.

Operator: Right, so you expect her home, what at, er, 4 o'clock then?

Karen: About half past three.

Operator: Right, does she have a mobile or anything like that?

Karen: No, it's at home.

Operator: Right, so we have no way of actually ringing to find out?

Karen: No.

Operator: And you have gone round all her friends and you have been in touch with all her relatives.

Karen: Yeh.

Operator: And there is nowhere else you have got left to look?

Karen: No.

Operator: Have you been in touch with school, if they can confirm that she's been to school?

Karen: She left school at normal time, at ten past three.

Operator: Right, what do they call her?

Karen: Shannon Matthews.
Operator: Has she been missing before?
Karen: No, first time.
Operator: And there's been nothing intimated why she should go?
Karen: No, not at all.

The recording is almost an Oscar-winning performance by Karen. When asked where she had been to check for Shannon, she instantly answered 'friends and family'. And when the operator asked if Shannon had a mobile phone she replied that it was still at home, without missing a beat to a question that might have caught out a more poorly prepared faker. Towards the end of the call, Karen's voice became choked with emotion as she appeared to fight back tears, apparently thinking about what might have happened to her daughter.

Because Shannon was just nine years old and had never gone missing before, she became a top priority for the police. Within 15 minutes, a squad car was outside Karen's home and PCs Andrew Blanchfield and Melissa Chessman Ward were knocking on the door, ready to start the search. The temperature had fallen to just above freezing and the officers were all too aware that it was a race against time if they were to find Shannon safely in these conditions. Potentially fatal hypothermia would be a real risk to anyone staying out in the extreme cold overnight.

The officers were greeted by Craig and three of Karen's other children: her 12-year-old and 5-year-old sons and her 2-year-old daughter. But Karen was nowhere to be seen – she was allegedly out searching for Shannon. When she returned shortly afterwards, Karen repeated the story of how Shannon had set off for school, frantically excited about her swimming lesson but then had simply never returned home. She seemed convinced her daughter must be 'out there' somewhere and pleaded with officers to help find her.

'She seemed very upset and shaky,' recalled PC Blanchfield. 'She was slightly crying; she said Shannon may have run away because her brother had received a computer from school, she said Shannon might be jealous that he had been given it.'

But PCs Blanchfield and Ward soon got a taste of what officers would be up against during the inquiry when Craig and Neil Hyett, who were also at the house, began acting aggressively towards them.

As PC Blanchfield stretched on a pair of blue latex gloves to begin searching the house for any clues Shannon might have left if she had run away, Craig started yelling, 'What are you accusing us of?'

The situation took a few minutes to calm down before the search could really begin. In the hours that followed, neighbours poured into the house to comfort Karen 'in her hour of need'. At times, she appeared close to tears as she repeated her story again and again of how Shannon had gone to school perfectly normally but never returned home.

The first stage of the police search that night was focused on tracing the route it was thought Shannon would have taken home. Officers then visited Leon Rose's home near Huddersfield to break the news that his daughter was missing and ask whether he'd had any recent contact with Shannon. Then immediate family and friends were called to see if any of them could think where Shannon might have gone had she run away.

The temperature dropped to minus four that night in Dewsbury – the lowest in Britain. With the wind chill factored in, it took it down to an achingly cold minus nine and weathermen were saying it was some of the coldest weather the county had known in years. But officers continued to painstakingly search local streets and parks. They were joined by locals, some of whom stayed out until dawn dressed only in tracksuits, with only their determination for the search to keep them warm – along with the endless brews of hot tea being handed out at the Dewsbury Moor Community House.

Men held torches and sticks as they roamed fields backing on to the estate, then retraced their steps back to the houses where they searched through bins, back gardens, lofts, sheds and garages – anything or anywhere that might yield some clue to where Shannon had gone. By dawn, when Shannon still hadn't returned home despite sub-zero temperatures, officers felt convinced this was no ordinary runaway case – no child could have endured that night out in the open, however much they may have wanted to teach their parent a lesson.

Fear that Shannon had been abducted was now foremost in officers' minds and the Homicide and Major Enquiry Team, led by Detective Superintendent Andy Brennan, was called in.

As a watery sun rose on the playing fields behind Dewsbury Moor on the morning of Wednesday, 20 February, it revealed a sharp frost across the grass. The sky was soon a bright shade of blue but it was bitingly cold for the residents who began to congregate on the estate's pavements, their faces masks of disbelief at the nightmare unfolding before them.

That day more than 200 police officers had been drafted in to support their Dewsbury colleagues already searching for Shannon. The West Yorkshire Police Training School in nearby Wakefield was temporarily closed down and cadets kitted out in padded fluorescent jackets were dispatched to join the hunt. Dozens more officers undertook house-to-house enquiries, questioning locals whether they had seen anything out of the ordinary in the past 24 hours.

A helicopter buzzed overhead, using heat-seeking technology to look for any signs of life in the wasteland below. In Crow Nest Park, rolling gardens of an old country house estate neighbouring Dewsbury Moor, mounted police scoured through undergrowth looking for any items of discarded clothing. Officers then sealed off a section of the park and broke the ice on a frozen lake before sending down underwater search teams into its dark, chill depths.

Later, a police cordon was set up on School Lane near where Shannon was last seen and officers searched flats near her home. Some initial sightings raised hopes that Shannon would be found quickly, safe and well. One witness said she was '100 per cent certain' she had seen Shannon since her disappearance. Another claimed to have seen her playing on school fields at around 7.30pm. But by the following day these sightings were being played down by police.

Other early reports of a girl matching Shannon's description – outside her school at 3.30pm, at a park by Staincliffe Road junction, and even at a local scrapyard – were also later ruled out. Detectives probed claims by one of the girl's schoolmates that he had heard her earlier the previous day saying she planned to run away. But it turned out to be a false lead.

As the day wore on, reporters from local newspapers – the *Dewsbury Reporter*, the *Batley News* and the larger regional *Yorkshire Evening Post* – were gradually joined by other journalists based in the north of England. The line of reporters' cars and outside-broadcast TV vans parked on Moorside Road lengthened with each passing hour, all eyes and lenses focused on the house at No 24, with its scrappy-looking grass and wind-lashed winter pansies. But there was no movement in or out for most of the day.

Detective Constable Christine Freeman had been assigned to be Karen Matthews's family liaison officer and she had collected Karen and Craig to keep them safe at the police station, away from the prying eyes of the media. Freeman, 51, was a single mum-of-three who had grown up just half a mile from Karen's home and knew the area inside out. 'I knew the parks where kids might go to hide and I was sure we'd find Shannon,' she said.

She also recalled her sense of trepidation at meeting a mother who would be going through such a terrible ordeal. 'As I walked up the path I didn't know what to expect,' said the policewoman. 'Hysterical tears? Screaming? Shouting? I shuddered as I remember how my eldest, now fighting in Iraq, had gone missing in the supermarket as a toddler. Luckily, he'd just wandered off, but I've never forgotten the terror I felt.'

But even on her very first visit to the house Det Con Freeman was left baffled by the atmosphere inside. Karen was slumped on the sofa, her eyes red and puffy as though she had spent the night crying. But Craig didn't even bother to look up from his Xbox.

Moments later, Det Con Freeman's telephone rang – her mobile-phone tune was a pop song her daughter had programmed in for her. The tringing tune filled the smoke-filled front room and suddenly Karen had leaped up from the settee and was dancing. 'I love this song!' she said.

The policewoman stared at the supposedly grief-stricken mother in confusion, then reminded herself how shock affects people in very different ways.

Officers spent time searching through Shannon's toys and possessions hoping she might have left some clue had she run away. They also took away Craig's computer from downstairs, which Shannon sometimes used, to check whether she had sparked up an online friendship which might have enticed her away. Karen and Craig were then whisked away from the media spotlight to the safety and security of Dewsbury Police Station.

In Karen's absence, friends and neighbours on Dewsbury Moor were more than happy to help reporters with their enquiries. Craig's sister and neighbour Amanda Hyett and her husband Neil painted a detailed picture of the missing girl for the waiting hacks. Amanda, a short, plump woman with a welcoming smile, appeared to be enjoying the media attention. But even the reporters were taken aback when Neil jokingly reminded his wife to charge 'a fiver for a feel' then roared with laughter, as they talked in the street.

Between the banter, Amanda described Shannon as a quiet, polite and friendly girl, who liked to stay in and play with dolls, make-up, computer games or her Bratz dolls. Amanda then told how she and Karen had spent the night searching the streets for Shannon. 'We weren't bothered about the cold, we just wanted to find Shannon,' she said, omitting details of the sat-nav and supermarket shopping expeditions. 'Thinking of Shannon out there in just her school uniform and coat is horrible,' she said.

Most of all, the waiting press pack were desperate for details of how Shannon's mother was coping with the nightmare. At the back of everyone's minds was the thought that here was a 'new Kate McCann', another mother wrongfully separated from her child and racked with torment.

Amanda was happy to oblige with detail. 'She is in a real state now, really upset,' she revealed. 'It is not like her daughter to go missing. It is something no parent wants to go through.'

Amanda's husband, a chunky well-built man with a moustache and closely cropped hair, told how he had been searching the streets for Shannon until 4.00am. 'We searched everywhere, driving around the whole area,' he said. 'We looked in neighbours' gardens and checked all the places she would normally be but came up with nothing. We're extremely worried. We're in limbo now and don't know what to do. It's completely out of character and unexpected for her to just go off. It's a horrible feeling that she might not even be in Yorkshire any more – she could be a million miles away by now if someone has her.

'She is a quiet girl and very shy – you might even say she is timid. If she had a problem she was not the kind of kid who would go running for help straight away. She is scared of the dark. That's why it's all a mystery.'

A picture was slowly emerging of Shannon but it was sketchy. All the descriptions kept returning to the words 'shy', 'timid' and 'scared' as if few people had really bothered to know her in any greater depth than that. Police started looking into reports among Shannon's friends that she had been talking about running away over recent weeks. But even close mates seemed to have little understanding of the sadness that had blighted Shannon's home life.

'Someone said they thought they saw her crying earlier in the day, though I was not aware of anything being wrong,' said one friend, Chloe West.

And no one was able to give the police any clue as to where she might have considered fleeing to, to escape from her unhappy home life.

During the afternoon, Chief Superintendent Barry South, Commander for the Kirklees area in which Dewsbury fell, called an emergency press conference near Shannon's school. It was now nearly 24 hours since she had been seen there when the coach dropped her off with her classmates. As the pack of reporters and TV crews gathered round, Chief Supt South delivered a bald statement. A serious-looking, thin-faced officer in his mid-forties and not given to great displays of emotion, Chief Supt South spoke deliberately and carefully as he told of his concerns for the missing child's welfare. 'Our priority at this moment in time is locating Shannon safe and well,' he said.

But there were few answers to the reporters' multitude of questions which followed about whether local sex offenders were being questioned and whether the inquiry was now being treated as an abduction. Whatever Chief Supt South's private theories about Shannon's fate, he wasn't letting them slip to the press. Statistics show that 96 per cent of abducted children are killed within 24 hours. And, no matter what Chief Supt South said publicly, he and his colleagues were well aware of that.

'Family members are devastated at this moment in time,'

Chief Supt South told the reporters. 'They are doing all they can to support us.'

But he could not have been more wrong. In fact, as darkness began to fall around teatime of the first full day of the search, the person who should have been most desperate to support the police inquiry was actually doing everything she could to obstruct it.

6

THE WORLD COMES
TO DEWSBURY MOOR

'Shannon, please come home,' Karen Matthews implored, looking towards the cameras, her eyes red, skin blotchy and pain seemingly seeping from her pores. No viewer of the evening television bulletins could have failed to be moved by the impassioned appeal at the end of the first full day's search for her missing daughter on Wednesday, 20 February.

With dark rings around her eyes and a voice seemingly sodden with tears, Karen Matthews appeared a broken woman and far, far older than her 32 years, as she returned home to Moorside Road that evening and made her impromptu television appeal. It was the first time she had been seen on screen and her sense of desperation was tangible even to people thousands of miles away.

'Shannon, you are not in trouble,' Karen pleaded. Then, seemingly too distraught to continue, she simply added, 'One thing Shannon does not like is dark and cold.'

It was very cold and very dark that evening and it was

now 30 hours since Shannon was last seen. The prospects looked bleak.

It was only later that it became apparent that Karen's depiction of pain was simply copied from the emotional outbursts she watched on *Jeremy Kyle*, rather than the real thing.

But to people watching from the comfort of their sofas at home that night, the agony in Karen's eyes, her shaking head and sense of desperation looked all too familiar – for months on end they had witnessed the same anguish in the face of Kate McCann, mother of missing Madeleine. However, despite the apparent similarities in the cases, on closer inspection there were few parallels between the families and circumstances of Madeleine McCann on holiday with her doting family in Portugal and Shannon Matthews, uncared for and neglected in Dewsbury.

But the thought that the same horror of a missing girl was unfolding all over again had an instant impact in homes and newsrooms across Britain. As a result, within minutes of the broadcast, any remaining newspapers, TV stations or national press agencies that didn't already have staff at the scene dispatched troops to Dewsbury Moor. Suddenly, everyone wanted to be part of the hunt for missing Shannon.

With the arrival of the press pack in earnest, Karen Matthews, her neighbours, the Dewsbury Moor estate and the entire town of Dewsbury were to find themselves scrutinised and judged in an unprecedented way. The initial verdicts of the press and TV teams were grim, with immediate comparisons with the TV show *Shameless* and adjectives such as 'run-down', 'sink' and 'slum' used as a prefix to almost every mention of the area.

Certainly, the estate – of which Moorside where Shannon lived was just one part – does suffer above the average number of criminal and social difficulties. In 2007, burglary affected 11.7 households per thousand, compared with 6.8 in Dewsbury itself and 5.4 across England and Wales. The same area has nearly three-quarters of its properties in the lowest council-tax band, none at all in the highest and only one each in the next two down.

Even from its earliest days, Dewsbury Moor had a reputation for roughness – a young curate was even sent to do 'mission work' among the tenants soon after its creation in the 1930s. The houses were built at the tail end of the 'Homes for Heroes' project – the plan to give working people who'd served in the First World War the opportunity to live in comfortable, modern houses surrounded by space and fresh air, far from the slums of the inner cities.

Dewsbury Moor was the dream of the rich aldermen of Dewsbury who, through their patronage, wanted to give the workers and poor of the town a better life. The city had grown rich beyond measure during the 19th century as the hub of Yorkshire's heavy wool industry, finding itself perfectly located on the banks of the new Calder and Hebble Navigation Canal and within easy reach of the vital coalfields.

Dewsbury's success came on the back of 'shoddy' – a textile term for rags used to make the local thick wool for blankets, rope and army uniforms. The 'shoddy' tag was to become a curse for the town, but, at the time, who cared? Everyone was far too busy enjoying full employment and widespread prosperity. An imposing town hall was built – and still stands as a reminder of those glory days – and money was ploughed into good works and improving the lot of the poor.

For the mill workers offered the chance to leave their terraced two-up, two-downs behind and move west up the Heckmondwike Road to the new houses being built for them on the Moor, it must have seemed like a dream come true. But it was always an odd place to build a new town, a collection of identikit semis superglued to the hillside where they are blasted day and night by the cold Yorkshire wind.

As you climb the road out of Dewsbury, past the beautifully preserved grounds of Crow Nest Park on the right, it feels as though you are striking out into a rural idyll straight from a Brontë novel – all wide open sky and untamed moorland, buffeted by the blustering winds. Charlotte Brontë even worked for a time just a stone's throw from Dewsbury Moor when she was employed as a teacher at a house now in the grounds of the district hospital.

Then with little warning you are in Dewsbury Moor and the sensation of wild, natural beauty is brutally stripped away with the appearance of a manmade sprawl of houses and shops, created with more emphasis on practicality than beauty. From the top of the estate, residents are treated to stunning views out across old mill chimneys and the houses below towards the moors, and in the very distance the foothill of the Pennines. The views make up for the bleaker aspect of looking closer at the estate where row after row of red-brick homes are lined up down the hillside.

For years after the estate was built, the residents would bus it into either Dewsbury in one direction or the Spen valley towns of Cleckheaton and Heckmondwike in the other, each of which then had different types of textile mills.

There was no shortage of jobs for the Moorsiders in those days, but, when manufacturing fell into decline, fewer and fewer residents were bussing it to work, and more and more were stranded at home, jobless and hopeless.

By the 1970s, bed manufacturing remained the town's only industry. Unemployment was high and the Moor's residents became almost cut adrift from their parent town below. Crime and yobbery flourished and many of Karen Matthews's generation grew up with no thought to ever landing a job. Infamy followed injustice and the biggest news in Dewsbury came in 1981 when serial killer Peter Sutcliffe, the Yorkshire Ripper, was questioned at the town's police station then formally charged before magistrates at the Town Hall.

During the late 1980s, as across the country, disused mills and industrial buildings were converted into swish new apartments and boutique shops. But the penthouses and chic little stores could have been a million miles from up the road in Dewsbury Moor. In the early 1990s, the reputation of Dewsbury was dealt another blow when it became linked with Islamic fundamentalism. The Markazi mosque became a centre for 4,000 worshippers and the European headquarters for Tablighi Jamaat, a group of revivalists who feared contamination of Islam as an embattled minority in the west. There was much concern that the town was becoming divided on racial lines.

Money and effort from the council and community groups was pumped into the area in a bid to get people living and working more closely together again. But all these good intentions were knocked sideways in the summer of 2007 when it emerged that Mohammad Sidique Khan, the ringleader of the 7/7 bombers in London, had been living in the town's Lees Holm area before carrying out his suicide mission.

But still the work to regenerate both Dewsbury and Dewsbury Moor continued apace. The Arts Council even chose Dewsbury as its HQ for Yorkshire and the Humber, and in 2007 the Dewsbury outdoor market was voted best in Britain. Up at Dewsbury Moor, a small fortune was pumped into the estate in a bid to improve the quality of life for its 5,650 residents, and robust policing was enforced to stamp out anti-social behaviour.

Just six years ago, the Moor had a reputation for fear and intimidation, with teenage gangs terrorising some residents and making lives a misery. Elderly people were too scared to leave home after dark because of yobs hanging around street corners, and young families were in constant fear of having their homes ransacked. It was also an almost entirely white-only district, putting it at odds with the wide ethnic mix across West Yorkshire. Dewsbury had one of the highest British National Party votes in the country, with party leader Nick Griffin calling it 'the jewel in our crown'.

One former resident, Zoe Porter, recalled the 'scum' days of the estate. 'Moorside had a terrible name,' she recalled. 'We'd houses burgled, sheds burned, caravans blown up!'

But, when raids, arrests and jail sentences broke one gang's reign of terror, life became easier for residents. More Asian families moved to the area, too, making it more representative of the social mix across Dewsbury.

Town planners also worked hard, spending more than £4 million on making Dewsbury Moor a better place to live for the tenants and owners of its 220 houses. Partly pedestrianised 'Home Zone' areas were created, designed to keep traffic speeds down, 'patrolled' by penguin-shaped bollards. Perhaps the town planners were having a laugh to themselves when they selected their Antarctic theme with so many penguins on the streets and children's play areas. As if washed up on some misdirected iceberg, the penguins have made the Moor their home. On some of the most bitter days during the hunt for Shannon, even they seemed to shiver.

Elsewhere, designer railings and boulders carved with ammonite fossils create the impression that much effort has gone into giving Dewsbury Moor pride in itself. Money was also spent on sprucing up the council houses with secure uPVC doors and windows being fitted, gates painted in bright colours, and crazy paving laid in the driveways.

Some tenants also took the opportunity to buy their own houses and have spent money on trying to individualise their homes from the others around them. Another huge step forward for Dewsbury Moor was the creation of its Tenants' and Residents' Association. One of the semis on the estate was turned over to become a Community House for the robust organisation and, under the leadership of formidable chairwoman Julie Bushby, it became a hub for the entire community.

Julie and her team of volunteers welcomed every new tenant, produced a bi-monthly newsletter and organised a full timetable of events for locals, from toddlers to the elderly. And after Shannon's disappearance it was the residents' group that coordinated search teams, offered support to the family and worked tirelessly to keep the hunt at the top of the news agenda day after day.

Dewsbury Moor is now far from its darkest days and there are many estates across Britain with far worse problems. But no one could claim it was some kind of new Eden at the time Shannon disappeared. Crime was still well above the national average and, although most families contain one worker, between 10 and 15 per cent of its working-age population survive on sickness or disability benefits. For those who are in employment, few earn above the minimum wage. Child mortality is also among the highest in the country, the result of bad diet, alcohol and smoking. And, while most tenants keep their homes looking reasonably neat and tidy, there are the telltale signs of neglect at others where gardens spill over with old mattresses, broken toys and waterlogged empty cardboard boxes. Biting winds sweep endlessly across the estate, and even at the height of summer it remains blustery and buffeted by the elements.

Despite the penguins and snazzy railings, Dewsbury Moor retains the aura of something forgotten and unloved. As if still lacking sufficient attention and affection, it has turned in on itself and grown cold and withdrawn. Almost like an unnoticed, uncared-for daughter of Dewsbury itself.

7

SHANNON,
'MY PRINCESS'

By first thing on Thursday, 21 February – Day Two of the hunt for Shannon – the line of reporters' cars and television vans stretched almost the full length of Moorside Road. Kids watched the live broadcasts with fascination on the way to school and locals chatted with reporters desperate to pick up a bit of local colour or inside family detail. From the scruffy suited agency hacks to the glossy-haired and brightly made-up television reporters, all forms of the nation's media were represented.

All eyes were focused on No 24 and the hope Karen Matthews might emerge again with another public appeal to find her daughter. But Karen and Craig were being kept away from the spotlight that day, and the job of making a public appeal went to Det Supt Andy Brennan, now heading up the inquiry into Shannon's disappearance.

Det Supt Brennan was tall and slim with angular features and a sober nature. As he addressed a packed press conference, it was clear he wasn't a man prone to exaggeration or hamming it up. His words sent out a sombre message: 'I could not be more concerned.'

Brennan was also too aware that, statistically, the chances of Shannon being found safe and well were slipping away by the minute. His best hope now was that a member of the public watching the appeal might remember some tiny detail they had previously overlooked or thought meaningless.

'This is a nine-year-old girl who has never been missing previously,' he said slowly. 'I would expect under normal circumstances we would have located her by now.' He said it was now believed she had a mobile phone with her but very little money and was not 'streetwise in any way, shape or form'. Asked if he had a message for her, he said, 'Shannon, you are not in trouble. We are genuinely concerned for you. Please contact your family or friends and we will come and collect you. You are not in any trouble at all.'

Detectives were investigating the row that had broken out at 24 Moorside Road the night before Shannon's disappearance when Shannon had been wrongly accused of taking money from Karen's purse. Local rumour had it that this argument had been 'the final straw' for Shannon and pushed her to run away.

If Shannon had disappeared voluntarily and was living somewhere out in the open or in a disused shed or garage, there were serious concerns for her health in the sub-zero temperatures Dewsbury had experienced over the last couple of nights. But senior detectives were increasingly convinced that this was far more than a case of a schoolgirl runaway. Even the most stubborn child would surely have been frozen home by now. And ordinarily there would have been numerous sightings of a girl out and about on her own at all times of the day and night. Most runaways return home or are found within the first 24 hours.

Shannon didn't fit the profile of a runaway either. She had never done it before, unlike her brother, and, given her age and timid nature, she couldn't have been further from the usual rebellious teenage runaway, desperate to teach their parents a lesson. Even supposing Shannon had run away, detectives were being drawn to the conclusion that she may have been snatched while out on the streets, vulnerable and alone.

Portuguese police had been pilloried for the seemingly unprofessional and disorganised investigation into the disappearance of Madeleine McCann – particularly in the critical first few hours. The West Yorkshire Police Force were determined that the same criticism would never be fired at them and they ensured no stone went unturned.

Hundreds of uniformed police, wrapped warmly in padded yellow fluorescent jackets, continued to trail from house to house, ensuring everyone on the estate was questioned. Reported sightings were checked out but none led to a concrete lead. By the end of the day, 200 homes had been visited. Meanwhile, other officers searched and re-searched sheds, garages, outhouses and bins. Others stretched out into a long line to carry out a fingertip search through nearby moorland.

A team of the county's most experienced detectives pursued other lines of enquiry. Work began on drawing up a family tree for Karen and Craig in the hope of identifying any potential abductors close to home. But this was no easy task, with one insider saying it looked more like a map of the London Underground than a family tree. Karen's mass of relationships meant all her exes and their families had to be included, as well as Craig's relatives too.

Another key line of enquiry was that Shannon might have been abducted by a paedophile. If this were the case, detectives knew they had hardly any time at all to locate her if she were to be found alive. Work was under way on sifting through the Sex Offenders' Register to locate all known paedophiles in the area. Again, it proved to be a massive task, with 302 registered sex offenders living in the area covered by Kirklees Council – 105 of which lived in Dewsbury itself. Each one of those had to be visited and interviewed before they could be ruled out.

While the checking and double-checking continued, Karen and Craig remained with police liaison officers, away from the TV cameras and on hand to answer any new questions detectives needed to check out. Det Con Christine Freeman spent that Thursday trying to learn more about Shannon in the hope that it would unearth some clue as to where she might have run to.

'What would you say to Shannon if she was naughty?' Det Con Freeman recalled asking Karen.

'I'd explain what she did wrong and ask her not to do it again,' Karen replied. She then went on to say how the family ate their dinner together every evening at the dining table – despite it being covered in junk and stuck in the corner of the room.

Det Con Freeman was uneasy. 'It was as if she was reading her answers out of the Good Parent Guide,' she recalled.

But why would Karen be lying? Maybe it was a sense of failure or guilt. And even if Karen wasn't a model parent that still didn't make her a child abductor.

But then something even more peculiar happened. Karen's eldest son went to the front door and appeared to be looking out at something. Then he yelled, 'Shannon's home!'

Det Con Freeman's heart leaped and started pounding. But Karen's eyes didn't even leave the television screen in the corner of the room. She didn't even glance towards the door. 'No, she's bloody not,' Karen finally snarled towards her son.

The teenager laughed back: 'Joke!'

Det Con Freeman felt a lurch of disappointment rip through her body. Then she considered Karen's extraordinary reaction to the sick joke. 'My mother's instinct screamed out, "This isn't right."'

It was around 7.30pm that evening that Karen made her second traumatic appeal for information about Shannon – in plenty of time for the late-night news bulletins. Wearing a grey hooded top, with her hair again scraped back, she looked sickly pale. Her eyes were red and her voice was quaking. 'If anyone's got my daughter, my beautiful princess daughter, bring her home, please,' she pleaded.

As she spoke, her voice trembled before she broke down sobbing. 'Shannon, you are a princess in every way, come home,' she said. 'We want her to come home safe. Me and her dad are missing her so much. Her older brother is going out of his mind and her little brothers and sisters just want her home safe.

'Shannon, if you're out there, please come home. We love you to bits, we miss you so much and love you so much. We have heard nothing from her, we just want her home with her family. If anyone has her, please return her. She's never ever done anything like this before. It's breaking everyone's heart to see her on the news.'

At times it felt like Karen's desperate pleading would never end – to viewers at home this was clearly a woman in torment. She may have struggled with her words and spoke in a rough, broad accent, but there was a rawness to her apparent grief which was agonising to watch. Struggling to speak, she then looked direct into one TV news camera, saying, 'Shannon, please come home, please I'm begging you baby, please come home,' before turning and rushing back into the house.

A short while later she returned, being supported by friends. 'If anyone's got my beautiful daughter just bring her back,' she continued. 'You're not in trouble and if you're hurt we'll do anything to help you. Shannon, please come home.'

But that night Det Supt Brennan and his team were no closer to bringing Shannon home than the moment she had disappeared. Morale and determination among the team remained high but they were in desperate need of a break.

By Day Three of the search – Friday, 22 February – there had been 250 calls to the police but only one sighting was still being seriously considered. More than 300 uniformed police, on foot and horseback, were combing a huge area of Dewsbury Moor and surrounding moorland. Fragments of clothes that could have belonged to Shannon were brought in evidence bags for Karen to examine, but nothing was familiar.

A specialist team had even plunged into freezing water in a storm drain using ropes and climbing equipment. Onlookers held their breath in anticipation they would resurface holding a body. But there was nothing. Sniffer dogs were taken backwards and forwards over the estate but failed to find any trace of Shannon's scent. There were now also 60 plain-clothes detectives from West Yorkshire CID investigating all possible leads and tip-offs. CCTV between Shannon's home and her dad's house in Dewsbury was analysed as were routes to other family members' homes. But still nothing.

Det Supt Brennan admitted he was 'surprised' by this. Normally, there would be something, *anything* that might at least hint as to Shannon's fate. But it really was beginning to feel as though she had vanished off the face of the earth.

In a bid to give the public a living image of Shannon that might jog memories, CCTV footage of her arriving and leaving Dewsbury Leisure Centre for the school swimming lesson was released. The image of the young girl, apparently happy and carefree, with no sense of what her fate held for her, shocked the nation when it was broadcast over and over on the news bulletins that night.

Shannon was seen leaving the leisure centre that afternoon, her shirt untucked like a million other young swimmers, as she swung her black coat around her shoulders before putting it on as she stepped out into the chill afternoon air.

At a press conference to release the footage, Det Supt Brennan also revealed the writing that had been on Shannon's wall: 'I want to live with my Dad'. In a bid to play down any significance it might hold, he went on to say that her bedroom walls were covered in 'childish scribblings'.

During a search of Shannon's bedroom, a note had also been found, written between Shannon and her brother – presumably when they were too scared to be heard talking. 'Do you think we'll get tea tonight?' asked one of the children in the note. 'We may get a packet of crisps if we keep quiet,' was the reply.

The note caused grave concerns among officers – but still did nothing to prove either Karen or Craig had anything to do with the abduction. But newspapers were already beginning to raise questions about the parenting skills of multiple mum Karen, and the revelation of Shannon's message on the bedroom wall only added fuel to the fire.

The scrawled message clearly had a devastating effect on Leon Rose, who seemed determined Shannon must have disappeared while making the ten-mile journey to his home. Leon, then jobless, had spent virtually every waking hour searching for his daughter. His face was puffy and waxy pale with dark circles around his eyes.

Perhaps Leon's fear for his daughter was compounded by a sense of guilt at not having seen Shannon for so long and being unaware how much she missed him. He certainly looked like a man who had lost much sleep thinking about the anguish his young daughter must have felt to write such a desperate message on her bedroom wall.

'I've been out and looked everywhere, I've just been searching,' Leon murmured to reporters. 'She's scared and cold and, basically, if someone's seen her I'd like them to ring the police straight away as soon as you see her so then we know where to look.' In a direct plea to Shannon, he said, 'If you can hear me, if you can get to the nearest phone box and ring 999 and tell them your name and they will be able to come and pick you up.'

But Karen was quick to make the point in an interview that Shannon had been happy at home and, contrary to the literal writing on the wall, she didn't want to go and live with her natural dad. 'She is really clingy with him,' said Karen referring to Craig, whom Shannon had also called Dad. 'She's a daddy's girl, more than a mummy's girl. On

Monday night, they were having tickling fights. They watched telly together and they would cuddle up together. She saw him as a dad and more as a father figure.'

Then Karen told how the only thing sustaining her was looking after her two-year-old daughter who had been kissing Shannon's picture in the newspapers. By then, Shannon's bed hadn't been slept in for three nights. Senior detectives felt it was time to brace Karen for the worst. It was the job every officer dreads.

Det Con Christine Freeman sat down with Karen and broke it to her gently that it was felt the chances were Shannon may not have made it. 'Do you understand?' the detective asked slowly.

Karen nodded hesitantly, but it was another hour before the tears started to flow. Then within seconds Karen had bolted to the door and was outside in front of the TV cameras again. 'I know my baby will come back to me,' Karen sobbed to the waiting reporters. It was a brilliant performance for an audience hungry for every morsel of emotion that could be rung out of the situation.

In the midst of all this, the locals of Dewsbury Moor had burst into action with their own incredible campaign to find Shannon. Its HQ was Dewsbury Moor's Community House – this looked identical to the other red-brick semis on the estate except that its patch of grass out the front had been paved over. Usually it was used for routine community events and meetings, planning summer picnics and outings for the kids, day trips for the elderly, the Halloween disco and, of course, the estate's annual August gala. It was the hub of the estate, the glue which kept the Moor's community together in good times and in bad. And this time it was as bad as it got.

During Shannon's disappearance, the Community House became like the frontline operations room of an army at war – maps lined the walls, piles of posters and leaflets filled every bit of floor space, a TV in the corner was constantly churning out footage from a rolling news channel and telephones rang incessantly. In a side room, a large stainless-steel tea urn produced out brew after brew for cold and tired searchers, leaflet distributors and general well-wishers doing what they could to help Karen and Craig.

At the heart of the Community House was plain-speaking, no-nonsense mum-of-three, Julie Bushby, chairperson of the Moorside Tenants' and Residents' Association. In the first few days, Julie helped organise search teams and liaised with the police as they launched their inquiry. And in the days that followed she ferociously protected Karen and Craig from the barrage of press interest following their every move. At the same time, she masterminded a sophisticated media campaign, realising, as the McCanns had, that the best chance of finding a missing child is to keep their story at the top of the news agenda.

Julie organised a whip-round to buy torches for searchers and persuaded a local Asda to donate 100 T-shirts on to which she ironed the question 'Have you seen Shannon?' With help from a growing band of volunteers, she borrowed a photocopier from a copy shop down the road and had hundreds of posters and leaflets printed which were distributed across the county.

There was barely a front window or signpost in Dewsbury Moor which didn't bear the printed poster of Shannon's shy grin smiling slightly side-on to the camera, her dark hair held back off her face in a pink scrunchy band. Beneath it were printed the words: 'Have You Seen This Girl?'

Shannon, who for so long had been denied any attention or spotlight, was now everywhere. No one in Dewsbury could walk to the end of the road without seeing an image of the little girl who had been lost to them all. More posters were printed in Urdu and Hungarian to ensure all ethnic groups living in the district got the message.

Outside the Community House hung a giant poster bearing the message 'HELP FIND SHANNON', flanked by two identical pictures of the smiling little girl. Teams were organised to distribute thousands of leaflets appealing for information across Dewsbury and further afield to Leeds and Bradford. Everyone was pitching in. The posters and leaflets were printed for free by local businesses, while taxi firms donated minibuses to take the volunteers and the leaflets to Leeds' White Rose Shopping Centre and to Wakefield. Local cafes and shops also did their bit by handing out free tea and coffee to the search teams.

But Julie Bushby wasn't remotely surprised by the locals' reaction. This was exactly how she knew people in Dewsbury Moor would rally in a crisis. 'This is the type of neighbourhood this is,' said the mum-of-three who had lived in Dewsbury Moor for three years. 'It's been absolutely fantastic. People here are honest people, they don't make a fuss. If there is something needs doing they get on with it.'

And the job that had to be done was to get Shannon home.

By Day Four of the search, the army of volunteers set off for Leeds' Elland Road football ground and rugby league ground to hand out more leaflets to fans. Others were distributed in the city's shopping centre. There can have been few people in the city who didn't see Shannon's face that cold Saturday afternoon.

Neil Hyett, a lifelong Leeds fan, said, 'It just came to me what better way to reach up to 25,000 people than at Elland Road. You never know, there is always the possibility that someone there will have that bit of information we need. We are widening our search; some of us think she is still in the area, but you have to look at the possibility she has been picked up. If people are coming into Leeds from outside of the area there is always the chance that someone might have seen something or heard something.'

That weekend, posters were stuck to lampposts up to ten miles away. Leaflets distributed by volunteers in their 'Missing Shannon' T-shirts reached as far as Birmingham and North Wales. An appeal to local businesses was able to fund another 20,000 print run.

Dewsbury MP Shahid Malik praised the outstanding community spirit which had come to the fore in the search for Shannon, saying it was 'something of which we can all rightly be proud. It's a powerful signal of how much the community cares about Shannon and our desire to have her back home where she belongs.'

But, however much the community wanted Shannon home, they were no closer to achieving it.

Locals unused to church services joined regular worshippers on Sunday, 24 February – Day Five of the hunt – for the morning service at St James' Church in Heckmondwike, which was dedicated to Shannon, and prayers were said for her safe return. The Rev Simon Pitcher, who led the service, said, 'We lit a candle and we had a silence so we could pray for her family and for her safe return.'

Those prayers were repeated in churches and mosques across Dewsbury. And, if Shannon could have been found by prayers, hard work and goodwill alone, the people of Dewsbury Moor would have found her. Hour after hour of free time was ploughed into the campaign, but, as the search entered its second week, the group discovered the cost of mounting a high-profile campaign. Appeals went out in the local newspaper and television for donations to keep it going. There were printing costs, volunteers' expenses and the cost of holding public meetings.

Karen's cousin, Susan Howgate, had also come up with the idea of a ribbon campaign – just like the yellow ribbons worn for missing Madeleine. She distributed them around Dewsbury Moor and they were worn with pride – but again this involved hefty expense for people living on meagre incomes.

There was increasingly a deep sense of injustice that so little financial support had rolled in to help find Shannon compared to the huge amounts donated to the Missing Madeleine appeal. That weekend Madeleine's parents, Gerry and Kate, posted a message of support for Shannon's family on their blog. Again, the similarities – and differences – between the cases of the two little girls were spotlighted to the public.

But what no one could have guessed at that point was there was one key reason for the similarities – Shannon's disappearance had been modelled entirely on the tragic tale of missing Madeleine.

8

THE MADELEINE
LINKS

'No matter what has happened to Shannon, there can be no doubt she must be extremely vulnerable,' Gerry McCann wrote in his internet blog on the first weekend following Shannon's disappearance. 'We hope she is found safe and well very soon and returned to her family. Our thoughts and prayers are with her family.'

No parents in the country could have been hoping and praying harder for Karen Matthews at that time – because the McCanns more than any other parents had an all-too-real understanding of what it felt like to endure the pain of an abducted child. Madeleine McCann was a pretty, lively three-year-old when she was abducted from a holiday apartment in the Portuguese resort of Praia de Luz on 3 May 2007.

The McCanns had put Madeleine and their younger twins, Sean and Amelie, to bed at the Mark Warner holiday resort where they were staying, then gone for dinner with friends at a restaurant on the complex just over 100 yards away. When they returned to check on the children at 10.00pm, Madeleine was missing. She has not been seen since, despite a mammoth search which has involved a publicity campaign propelled by the determination of the McCanns to find their daughter.

The case of Madeleine McCann dominated the news agenda in Britain, Europe and even the United States throughout the summer and most of the autumn of 2007. There had rarely been a story which seemed to attract such a huge amount of attention for such a long period of time.

The British public followed every twist and turn of the story through the initial shock of the little girl's disappearance, the public debate on whether the McCanns should have left such young children alone, to the revelation and then elimination of various suspects.

It seemed a never-ending saga. But all the time – through all the public appeals, television appearances, newspaper interviews and general furore – donations kept flooding in for the Find Madeleine Fund. The fund has received more than £2.5 million since Madeleine's disappearance, and at the time of writing this has been almost entirely spent in the ongoing hunt.

In addition, within a fortnight of the abduction, rewards totalling another £2.5 million had been offered by newspapers, television networks and private donors. Virtually no one in Britain could have missed the attention surrounding the Madeleine McCann case and the generosity from ordinary people that it prompted.

Karen Matthews – with her 18-hour-a-day TV habit – was particularly well informed about what had gone on. And it was this, many detectives believe, that first planted the idea in her mind for staging the disappearance of her own daughter. After the conclusion of the trial, Det Supt Andy Brennan revealed his thoughts on the links between the cases.

'Clearly, the McCann case was still in everybody's mind,' he recalled. 'Madeleine McCann gave them the idea – the fund money. Shannon was chosen instead of her brother because she was a girl and more photogenic.

'I believe they were trying to get £50,000, that's supported by the newspapers in the flat and the comments of Donovan. I don't believe everything he says, but I believe he was motivated by the desire to get money. Where Karen Matthews is concerned, if it was the money or Shannon, the money would always have won. I think it's really sad because it's the one person Shannon should have been able to trust.'

Perhaps Karen thought that Shannon, unlike her elder brother, would win greater public sympathy when her quiet, timid nature became known. Karen's youngest child – her two-year-old daughter – was also ruled out, presumably because she would have been harder to keep quiet and under control during the long period of incarceration.

From Karen's first meeting with Michael Donovan at the Dewsbury café where she issued him with his orders for the plot, it seems she was confident a reward would be offered by a newspaper for her daughter's safe return. The money would enable her to pay off her loans and treat herself to some of the eBay bargains she spent her days perusing. Then it seems she believed life for them – including Shannon – would simply slip back to normal.

So Karen must have been concerned when, for the first 24 hours of Shannon's disappearance, the story received little attention outside the local and regional press. Local newspapers in Dewsbury and then Leeds and Halifax picked up the story immediately but there was initially little mention in the national tabloids or television bulletins.

Then Karen made her first tearful front-gate appeal outside 24 Moorside Road – and the media was hooked. Karen had watched enough television to know exactly what the cameras required in this situation: an anguish-filled mother struggling to keep it together. Her performance did not disappoint.

In the days that followed, twists and turns of the case were monitored closely in the papers with much analysis devoted to the rundown nature of the Dewsbury Moor estate, and not to mention Karen Matthews's complicated home life. A week after her disappearance, it seemed that Shannon was well on her way to filling the vacuum left on the front pages by the finally waning interest in the McCann case. It all seemed to be working out just as Karen Matthews had hoped and she continued to fuel the interest with regular impromptu appeals to the cameras.

Karen Matthews may have had a pitifully low IQ but she had enough streetwise nous to have conned social workers and the Benefits Office over the years. And she certainly had the wit to know what was required in her TV role as 'grieving mother'.

Firstly, she chose her moments for the television appeals and knew how to hit the nation's sympathy button – albeit hers had the backdrop of windswept Dewsbury rather than sun-bleached Praia de Luz. And, instead of the slim, attractive figure of Kate McCann in discreet make-up and freshly laundered clothes, there was Karen Matthews lumbering on to screens in a football shirt and parka jacket.

But some might argue Karen Matthews performed her TV appeals far better than Kate McCann who had been advised by police not to show emotion, and as a result many viewers believed her to be aloof. In contrast, Karen's red-rimmed eyes, untamed hair and uncontrollable sobs made many viewers feel she must be the 'real deal'. Some believe Karen lacked the intelligence to know exactly how to hoodwink the police, media and public for so long. But she knew that tears, anger and agony were exactly what the public wanted to see.

Nine months after Madeleine's disappearance, the McCanns had become fair game for many in the media. Even Karen Matthews must have picked up on the comments made of them for coldness and clinical professionalism in their campaign. Karen ensured – either deliberately or by accident – that no such accusations could be thrown at her. Meanwhile, she also played up all the similarities between the Shannon and Madeleine cases. There were many subtle parallels that Karen used to her advantage. Kate McCann had been seen holding and smelling her daughter's favourite soft toy, Cuddle Cat. Karen Matthews posed at a press conference with a 'Love Teddy' which she claimed had been Shannon's favourite. But, while Kate McCann had clung on to the Cuddle Cat in desperation, week after week, holding it to her face, smelling its familiar scent and hugging it the way her daughter had, Karen looked strangely awkward as she held the little teddy to her shoulder.

In another similarity, the McCanns had told how their twins kept asking when their older sister Madeleine was coming home and where she had gone to. Karen Matthews told reporters that her two-year-old daughter thought

Shannon was on holiday and kept asking when it would be time for her to return.

There were even parallels between the language Karen and the McCanns used. During Shannon's disappearance, Karen repeatedly referred to her as her 'beautiful princess' and 'little princess'. Could she have remembered that, just four months earlier, Gerry McCann had said, 'We have no idea whether she is suffering but we have to hope and pray that she is being treated like a princess, as she deserves'?

Certainly, Karen wasted no time in responding to the McCanns' message of support sent the first weekend after Shannon's disappearance. 'I'm really touched that another family who are going through the same thing are thinking and praying for us,' she said.

She was so touched, in fact, that within two days a message had been sent from Craig Meehan's computer to the Find Madeleine Fund, demanding that money be shared with Shannon's less starry campaign. Further requests from the fund followed by letter, email and telephone.

'We received a number of approaches either directly or indirectly from people purporting to be members of Shannon's family asking for donations from the Madeleine Fund,' recalled McCann family spokesman Clarence Mitchell.

One caller claimed to be a relative and another telephone appeal received by Mr Mitchell himself was from a woman claiming to be a friend of the family. 'She said Karen – Shannon's mum – wanted to speak to me. I heard a woman in the background saying, "No, no – you speak to him."'

Mr Mitchell said he was taken aback by the direct nature of the approach but promised to pass it on to the McCanns. 'At the time, Gerry and Kate understandably expressed sympathy with her family,' he said. 'The idea of making a donation was discussed by the fund's board of directors who considered helping out as an offer of goodwill.'

Kate McCann was particularly moved by Karen's distress and the thought that another little girl, so like her daughter, was now frightened, alone and far from her family. Kate was desperate to help but, before any money from the Find Madeleine Fund was raised, concerns started to grow about the increasing number and nature of requests being received from friends and family of Karen Matthews.

'They were quite blunt – saying things like: "Madeleine's family has got loads of money and we want some for Shannon,"' recalled Mr Mitchell. 'A man also turned up at Kate and Gerry's house one Sunday as they were about to leave to go to church. He banged on their door and asked if they would donate money from the fund to help Shannon's family.'

Still, the fund was poised to hand over £25,000 when the police advised them to hold back. Although Karen was still not a suspect, it was not felt advisable to be doling out great wads of cash to her. So the repeated appeals for cash were politely rejected, the official reason being that 'the fund had decided against getting involved'. No further explanation was given.

With cash failing to materialise from the Find Madeleine Fund, Karen had to look elsewhere. But, if she had been hoping for a huge influx of donations from the public, she was disappointed there too. Donations for Madeleine reached £1.1 million in just two weeks. For Shannon, it was 'thousands at best'. So Karen Matthews was left with just one hope – that her initial plan to land a £50,000 reward for her missing daughter would still come off. But even that wasn't going quite as she might have hoped.

When Ian Huntley's victims, Holly Wells and Jessica Chapman, went missing in the Cambridgeshire village of Soham in August 2002, there was a £1 million reward for information put up by two tabloid newspapers within just a few days. But for Shannon, it took until Day 11 of the search before the *Sun* newspaper pitched in with a paltry £20,000 reward – less than half the figure Karen had been banking on.

And even worse for Karen was that, rather than gaining momentum, the story was starting to drift off the front pages into smaller stories inside the tabloids. At the same time, live TV reports from Dewsbury Moor were being shunted from the national to the regional television bulletins.

There was also a lack of the outpouring of celebrity emotion that so often follows national tragedies or crimes. Premiership footballers, television celebrities and high-profile businesspeople had all offered public backing and financial assistance to Madeleine's parents. The only star-studded support for Karen Matthews came in the form of a statement released through the management company of *X Factor* winner Leona Lewis.

This really wasn't how Karen had planned it at all. But then Shannon's new neglect at the hands of the popular press led to an outpouring of hand-wringing by media watchers and social commentators. The same questions were repeated again and again: why had the level of press interest in Shannon's case collapsed so soon compared with the ongoing fascination with the Madeleine McCann case?

Was one girl's life simply worth more than another's? And, if so, did it all come down to class? Madeleine

McCann's parents were doctors who lived in a well-heeled Leicestershire village. Shannon Matthews's mother had seven kids by six men, had barely worked a day in her life and lived on a grim-looking council estate. For many, the missing girls seemed to symbolise the huge social divisions existing within Britain.

For those violently opposed to the British class structure, Karen Matthews represented the tragic oppressed. The McCanns were the wealthy middle classes. Left-wing writer Beatrix Campbell summed up that mood in a piece for the *Guardian*: 'Karen Matthews has acted appropriately throughout. She was waiting for Shannon at home; she contacted the police as soon as she had exhausted all the obvious locations. And yet, our eye is drawn to her poverty, numbers of partners, cans of lager going into her household. Everything about Ms Matthews' life has been up for scrutiny.'

By contrast, Beatrix Campbell claimed, the McCanns' 'resources – money, looks, religion, organisation, focus (all a function of class)' had been mobilised

Media commentator Roy Greenslade also put it down to class. He wrote: 'In "respectable" working class eyes, she [Karen Matthews] would be regarded as a member of the underclass and, by implication, the author of her own misfortunes. Unlike the supposedly middle-class McCann family, with their "respectable" careers in medicine, Karen lacks eloquence. Neither she nor her daughter is photogenic.

'There are not "cute" pictures of the girl and no video of her. The absence of moving images is particularly important for TV coverage, of course. The repetition of clips of attractive victims of crime is a common feature of TV news bulletins.'

So again it appeared that little Shannon Matthews was being neglected – this time by the press. Tragically, she just wasn't rich, cute, quirky or from a sufficiently middle-class family to sustain national interest for very long. Even the McCanns themselves appealed for more attention for the Shannon case. A spokesman for the family told reporters, 'Shannon is a vulnerable missing child and we'd hope that the media would focus on her situation and cover her plight in as wide and balanced a way as possible.'

It is unclear how aware Karen Matthews was of the class prejudices which were obstructing her quest to keep her daughter on the front pages. But at some instinctive level she fully understood the differences between herself and the McCanns and played on prejudices against the couple that had become prevalent in some areas – that they were too uptight, too slick in their media campaign and too perfect in their domestic life with their professional careers, Mark Warner holidays and friends dining on tapas.

She wanted to impress the similarities of shared tragedy and loss but also record the inequalities of attention and resources for the campaign. She was asked repeatedly how she felt about being compared with the McCanns. To one reporter she said, 'They are nothing like us, they're snobs,' although to uneducated Karen maybe by using the word 'snobs' she simply meant middle class.

Craig chipped in too: 'We shouldn't be compared to them, because they are celebrities in other people's eyes and they have all the money. It is a bit ridiculous.'

During the hunt for Shannon, some posters even made direct reference to the Madeleine campaign. 'We are just like them, though their campaign is rich and, to be honest, we haven't got a lot here.'

Sadly, though, for the honest people of Dewsbury Moor, who worked so tirelessly in the hunt and who donated to it much of their small incomes, the real abduction of Madeleine and faked disappearance of Shannon could not have been more different.

9

'WE WANT YOU HOME'

Parents in Dewsbury Moor were facing up to the idea that somewhere near their home, even among their neighbours, there could be a child abductor, watching and waiting. Or, if not, there was the equally troubling thought that someone had appeared from outside, snatched a child unnoticed from the street, then left again. And if they had done it once, what was to stop them doing it again? An atmosphere of fear crept on to the estate.

At first the adrenalin of the search, the poster campaign and the novelty of the nation's press camped on their doorstep had shielded many residents from the reality of Shannon's abduction. But now that terrible reality was hitting home – and hard. During the day, parents wearing 'Have You Seen Shannon?' T-shirts held the hands of their children that little bit firmer as they dropped them at school.

Later, the normally noisy playing fields behind Moorside Road stood silent and still as dusk crept up the hillside.

And, when streetlights burst into the gloom, curtains were firmly pulled – the people of Dewsbury Moor were intent on keeping from their homes the evil they now feared was lurking outside. The sense of eeriness had been exacerbated by another horrific incident on Dewsbury Moor – the crucifixion of a local man.

On the Sunday following Shannon's disappearance, the 43-year-old was discovered by a neighbour in wasteland just yards from her home. He was lying on the ground on a wooden cross to which his hands had been nailed. The horrified woman who found him, recalled, 'I was leaving my neighbour's house at 11.45pm when I heard him singing. I told him to get up, thinking he was drunk, but he cried, "I can't."

'My nephew Mark shouted, "Get over here, he's nailed to some wood, I've called an ambulance."'

But as the scared woman moved closer to the victim, she realised it wasn't just wood – it was a cross. The victim claimed someone had dragged him from his home then carried out the crucifixion.

Many locals were convinced the incident must be linked to Shannon's disappearance and the rumour mill went into overdrive. Some believed it to be a lynching-style revenge and therefore the man must have had something to do with Shannon's abduction. Others wondered if he had information about the missing girl's whereabouts and was being silenced by her captors.

Either way, the police denied any link between the crucifixion and Shannon's disappearance. Rather, they seemed content it was just another curious event in the daily goings-on on Dewsbury Moor. The man was never identified and was moved away from the estate before anyone could fully get to the bottom of what had happened that day.

In the immediate aftermath, though, the crucifixion incident only added to the sense of fear felt by many locals on the estate. But such concerns were not troubling Karen Matthews. Because she, of all people, knew there was still very little to fear in Dewsbury Moor beyond the petty crime which had always troubled it.

In one of her regular updates to waiting reporters, Amanda Hyett said Karen was 'bearing up well given the circumstances'. And indeed she was. Karen and Craig had moved into the home of their friends and neighbours, Natalie and Peter Brown, so a full forensic search could be carried out at their home in the hope it might shed light on where Shannon had gone.

Natalie, a 28-year-old mum-of-four, had willingly offered to take in the couple and their kids for five days during their time of need. But quite soon she and husband Peter – a former soldier – became confused by the sudden swings in Karen's moods and strange incidents in her behaviour. Karen helped out Natalie around the house, made cuppas when it was her turn and generally made herself at home. So much so, in fact, that at times Natalie found it difficult to detect any change in her at all since Shannon's disappearance.

She continued to watch hours of television and computer games and laughed and play-fought with Craig. 'We would laugh and joke about day-to-day things the kids were doing. It was like a normal conversation,' Natalie later recalled in court. 'One minute she would be laughing and be happy and joking but when news came on TV she would be very quiet and not talk.'

One day, a news programme was on in the house and a picture of Shannon appeared on the screen. Karen turned to her two-year-old daughter sitting next to her on the sofa and shouted, 'Look, Shannon is on TV! She's famous!'

It was Natalie who had to remind her, 'She's not famous. She's missing.'

Another television report mentioned that Karen had had five husbands. 'That's a f****** lie,' Karen screamed at the television set. 'I never married any of 'em.'

On another occasion, Karen, Natalie and some other girlfriends started talking about a young police officer on duty outside the house. 'He's got a really cute bum,' one of the women laughed to the group.

But Karen was happy to take the joke further. 'I wouldn't mind taking him upstairs,' she giggled to her pals.

Even her closest friends were quietly shocked Karen could be comfortable making crude jokes at such a terrible time in her life. Worry was having little impact on Karen's appetite either and she was still regularly wolfing down her favourite takeaway supper of fish and chips with curry sauce, even though most people in such a situation would have barely been able to eat at all.

Natalie also became aware how Karen's normally upbeat mood would alter once her police liaison officers arrived. Then she would go 'really quiet', offering simply 'yes' or 'no' answers to their questions. Asked how Ms Matthews was when police were not around, she replied, 'It was like Jekyll and Hyde.'

'I saw her after she left my house,' said Natalie. 'When the police or the press were there she came over as if she was all upset and withdrawn, but when they were not there she would be back to her usual self, having a laugh and joke and having normal conversations with everybody.'

In fact, in all the time Karen stayed with the Browns, Natalie never once saw what she thought were real tears.

Even at an action meeting to plan the next stage of the funding and publicity for the 'Find Shannon' campaign at the Moorside Community House, Karen was seen laughing and joking. But for the searchers still combing Dewsbury Moor in the perishing cold there was little to laugh about.

Karen and Craig – who'd been given compassionate leave by Morrisons – spent hours at the Community House, chatting and sharing cigarettes. Craig would down endless cans of Coke while Karen drank tea and watched the rolling news channel being screened in a corner of the room. But while other residents pored over search maps and organised leaflet drops, Karen appeared strangely disinterested in the efforts going on to find her daughter.

On Day Six of the search – Monday, 25 February – 50 specialist police officers dressed in protective suits and face masks began searching bins all along routes Shannon could have taken home from school. They were joined by council binmen who sifted through trash hoping to find an item of clothing that would provide a lead. Sewers and gullies were inspected and a pond behind nearby Dewsbury Hospital was dredged.

Roadblocks were instituted all around Dewsbury and thousands of cars were stopped in long lines by yellow-coated officers holding clipboards and buffeted by the wind. Officers then quizzed drivers, digging away for the tiniest shred of information or slightest recollection of 19 February, the day Shannon disappeared.

Searches of garages, workshops, business units and

homes continued too. More than 200 homes within half a mile of Moorside Road had been searched and more than 300 calls from the public received. The hunt was at its peak. One in ten officers from the entire West Yorkshire Police Force were involved in looking for Shannon but they were still no closer to finding her.

Day after freezing day the hunt continued. For the searchers, it must have felt as though spring was never going to come. On Tuesday, 26 February, it was one week since Shannon had disappeared. Police and neighbours on Dewsbury Moor all feared the worst.

Det Supt Brennan called a press conference against the inauspicious backdrop of Dewsbury Moor crematorium. The mood was sombre as he explained a shift in emphasis of the inquiry. He conceded the possibility that Shannon had been abducted was now one theory being considered by his team, which he revealed was now operating an inquiry more along the lines of a murder-style investigation. 'What concerns me greatly is that Shannon, a vulnerable nine-year-old girl, may have fallen into the wrong hands,' he said.

'We are using all available technology and expertise including behavioural experts and a team of dedicated scientists. While we hope and pray that Shannon will be found safe and well, we remain gravely concerned. I'm convinced that, if Shannon had run away that night of her own volition, in a den or hideaway of some sort, we would have found her by now – a week on from when the investigation opened.

'It is very rare in searches of this kind that a girl of Shannon's age should be missing for this long without any clues pointing to her whereabouts. It is extremely concerning and we are now looking at this on a scale as serious as a murder investigation.

'It can now be said that the tone of our inquiry has changed to a bleaker outlook. The shift in emphasis is that we are now looking for individuals who may have been seen on the day of her disappearance, acting suspiciously, or unknown to the local community.'

In a bid to keep the story alive in people's minds, two fresh pictures of Shannon were released. In one she sat in a grassy meadow, smiling at the camera with her dog Scania lying protectively in front of her. In another she was stretching to blow out candles on her ninth birthday cake the previous September. Few people could have seen that picture without wondering if Shannon would ever blow out birthday candles again.

Ten miles away, the home of Shannon's dad, Leon Rose, was searched. He too was clearly feeling the strain. 'Every day since she went missing has been an absolute nightmare,' he said. 'I just hope she's not dead. I don't want to find her at the bottom of a pond. I don't want to fear the worst. I'd rather be driving down the road and see her walking along.'

Fingertip searches were by now under way at every house in Moorside Road. A dozen police officers, with white masks covering their mouths, rummaged through rubbish in gardens and inside the homes. The home of one of Karen's ex-boyfriends was searched, as was Neil and Amanda Hyett's.

Just 50 minutes later, officers left the Hyetts' house, apparently empty-handed. They moved on quietly and methodically to the next house on their list in what appeared an increasingly fruitless quest.

More than 500 items of property had been discovered or handed in during that first week which officers thought might offer a lead as to Shannon's whereabouts. None of them did. Even the mountain rescue teams and specialist dog units, trained to find bodies in the most difficult environments, had failed to find a lead. As had anti-terror officers, seconded to analyse CCTV footage.

Thoughts that Shannon's disappearance might have been linked to the attempted abduction of a 12-year-old girl seven miles away in Wakefield on the same day were also ruled out. Nothing seemed to link, connect or point to a reason for Shannon's disappearance.

There seemed a forlorn look on every face in Dewsbury Moor that Tuesday, the whirr of a police helicopter circling above the estate only adding to the sense of gloom.

To mark the first week of Shannon's disappearance, prayers were said for her and candles lit at Saint John The Baptist Church in Dewsbury. Then, as the sun started to set over the playing fields where Shannon had played a thousand times, the locals of Dewsbury Moor held a candlelit vigil for her. They called it 'A Walk for Shannon' and locals joined in their droves. About 300 people – white and Asian, young and old – turned out that wild and windy evening, gathering outside the Moorside Tenants' and Residents' Association house.

When Karen and Craig appeared and took their place at the front of the walkers, a spontaneous wave of applause swept through the crowd. Karen looked tired and pale – the perfect picture of a mother in anguish. The walkers set off from the Community House and slowly wound their way the 300 yards to Shannon's home.

At the front, Shannon's shy smile beamed out from a

huge banner. Behind it were Karen and Craig, wearing large white T-shirts bearing the message 'Have you seen Shannon Matthews?' They stuck close together, their heads sometimes bowed against the cold evening air. Behind them, elderly people walked arm-in-arm with their young neighbours. Kids on bikes joined at the back and even babies and toddlers were pushed along in their buggies.

As the group trudged along, the friends sang, 'It's Love that Makes the World Go Round', which Shannon's schoolfriends said had been one of her favourites. After a while, the singing faded into a simple chant: 'Shannon, we want you home'. And then it was just the united sound of 300 voices calling 'Shannon', 'Shannon', 'Shannon' into the night air, as if by some miracle she might still be able to hear them.

Karen joined in those desperate calls, repeating her daughter's name as friends, neighbours and total strangers watched her, overwhelmed by her apparent strength and horrified by her loss.

When the group arrived outside 24 Moorside Road, children released hundreds of colourful balloons into the air, each one bearing a personal message of hope for Shannon and her family. Among the schoolkids was little Megan Aldridge, Shannon's best friend. At times the sadness of the situation overcame her and tears ran down her face. Then other children laid winter flowers on the grass at the front of the house.

On a bleak and blustery night, it was a beautiful ceremony full of hope which showed the true compassion of the people of Dewsbury Moor. At the door of the house, Karen paused briefly for pictures before quickly slipping inside with the three remaining children.

Outside, the gathered walkers seemed reluctant to leave – they didn't want it to be over, this feeling of doing something for Shannon. Instead, they stood and prayed quietly for the missing girl. The Rev Canon Kevin Partington, Rector of Dewsbury, thanked the crowd for coming out on a cold and windy night and said, 'We are all here to show our love and support for Shannon and her family. All our prayers are with them. It's a really significant night for the community on the first-week anniversary of her disappearance.'

Julie Bushby, who had organised the walk, also thanked locals for turning out. She explained how it was the first time Karen had been able to see for herself the incredible support for her in the local estates. 'She knows now that the community is there for her,' she said.

The Rev Kathy Robertson, the newly installed vicar designate at the local St John's Church, said it was vital to 'stand and walk with the community'. She then summed up the event simply, saying, 'We all want Shannon home and we want to express that to her.'

The evening had been so full of hope that it made the following morning all the harder to bear when nothing the police could report gave any foundation for that hope at all.

It may have been only a week since she last stepped out of that heavy front door, but to many of the local people of Dewsbury Moor it felt like a lifetime. Shannon's schoolfriends were all keen to help the search and some young people on the estate had the idea of setting up a Facebook page in her name. A staggering 8,000 people joined the 'Help Find Shannon Matthews' group.

Meanwhile, videos made from still photographs of

Shannon released by her family were popping up on YouTube. One video had a montage of Shannon pictures and messages of hope set to the song 'Beautiful Soul'. The opening message was written in text speak: 'Shannon bayb33 if your out th3re com3 hom3 plz'. Thousands of people viewed the video and many replied with personal messages of support.

As that week wore on, Craig and Karen spent more and more time at the Moorside Community House. There they could feel at the centre of events and were looked after constantly by the campaign group with cups of tea and butties to keep their strength up. 'They are doing as well as they can, considering what they are going through,' Julie Bushby said at the time.

The campaign received a huge publicity boost on Day Nine of the search – Thursday, 28 February – when chart-topping *X Factor* star Leona Lewis sent her personal message to Shannon and her family. Leona spoke out after being told her single 'Bleeding Love' was Shannon's favourite song. Karen must have loved the celebrity attention while presumably giving little thought as to why a nine-year-old would be so attached to a song which starts with the line: 'Closed off from love, I don't need the pain.'

In her statement, Leona said, 'My heart goes out to Shannon's family at such a painful time. I urge anyone to come forward if they know anything about this.' She then added a direct message to Shannon: 'If Shannon is reading this, then I urge her to get in touch with her parents and come home.'

The publicity must have been welcome for Karen who was surely beginning to seriously worry that there had still been no reward for Shannon's safe return.

On Day Ten – Friday, 29 February – best friend Megan Aldridge spoke of her sadness at life without Shannon. The pair, who had been together on the school bus on the way to swimming and back again, had been inseparable for months. 'Please come home Shannon,' Megan said. 'We all miss you.'

Megan's dad, Mark Aldridge, said his daughter had been distraught since Shannon's disappearance. 'Every day has been hard for Megan,' he said. 'She finds it hard to make friends, but she had two. One of them has gone to Australia and now Shannon has disappeared. It is unbelievable. Since it happened Megan has been having trouble sleeping and she is finding it hard at school.'

The dad-of-two said he had been left chilled by the CCTV images of Shannon's last-known movements. 'Those pictures of Shannon walking into Dewsbury Sports Centre, that is Megan at the side of her,' he said. 'They are that close, they were nearly always together. You can't help wonder what has happened.'

Then, Huddersfield firm Joseph Furniture, which had once employed Neil Hyett, stepped in with a £5,000 reward. Not quite the figure Karen had envisaged but she must have been getting desperate. In a statement, bosses of Joseph Furniture, said, 'As a company that was founded in Dewsbury, we feel a social and moral responsibility to aid with reuniting Shannon Matthews with her beloved family.'

Karen must have been desperately hoping that other local businesses and newspapers might follow the generous lead. Certainly, she was enjoying the spontaneous generous gestures of the public – many of whom were sending cash in the post, some simply addressed to 'Karen Matthews, Dewsbury'.

Every day envelopes filled with pretty cards and £10, £20 and even £50 notes dropped through the letterbox. 'Once I was round there and a fat brown envelope came through the letterbox,' Amanda Hyett recalled later. 'I picked it up off the dirty floor but Karen snatched it from me like an animal and tore it open. There was a wad of notes in there along with a card from someone wanting to help with the appeal. Karen was like a kid at Christmas when she saw the money. It went straight into her pocket.'

But the big tens-of-thousands rewards Karen had hoped for had still not materialised. Instead, day after day slipped by, each with a different appeal for information, each feeling a little more desperate than the last.

At first, nobody in Dewsbury Moor had dared voice the concerns they buried deep down – that Shannon might have been abducted and murdered. But as the days came and went and still there was no sign of her, the fears were raised, first quietly, then publicly and then again and again as people teased away at the problem, talking through all the possible conclusions.

Many local people still clearly remembered the cases of Sarah Harper and Leanne Tiernan who had both disappeared from their homes eight miles away, near Leeds. Those cases had both started out as missing-child inquiries too before it was revealed the girls had been abducted and murdered by two different sexual predators.

Choirgirl Sarah Harper was just a year older than Shannon when she disappeared on her way to a local shop in Morley, near Leeds, in March 1986. Her body was found in the River Trent in Nottinghamshire the following month. Then, in November 2000, 16-year-old Leanne Tiernan was snatched as she walked along an unlit wooded path near her home in nearby Bramley. It was another nine months before her body was found buried in a shallow grave near Otley.

Sarah's killer turned out to be serial killer Robert Black, from North London. He snatched and killed at least two other young girls while travelling the country as a delivery driver. He was given ten life sentences in 1994. Leanne's murderer, John Taylor, of Leeds, was sentenced to a minimum of 30 years after admitting her murder in 2002.

Police officers on the Shannon inquiry looked back to the cases of Leanne Tiernan and Sarah Harper and the lessons they had learned from them. And local people across West Yorkshire reflected on the same cases and remembered the feelings of hopelessness and fear they'd had then – and were now feeling all over again.

Finally, ten long days after the disappearance of her daughter, Karen Matthews received the news she had been waiting for – not that Shannon had been found, but that the *Sun* newspaper had pitched in with a £20,000 reward. Even with the £5,000 from the Huddersfield furniture company, the total sum was just half what Karen had been hoping for, but it was still more than she had ever earned in her life before.

The *Sun*'s offer came with the proviso that it was: 'Subject to terms and conditions and Editor's discretion'. How Karen thought she was going to dupe the country's biggest-selling daily newspaper and end up pocketing the cash herself defies belief. Perhaps greed had overwhelmed any sense of reality.

The *Sun* also printed a full page 'Find Shannon' poster which it implored readers to place in their windows to help the search. Karen and Craig posed holding the poster, staring intently into the camera lens. 'I'm so grateful for all you are doing,' Karen said. 'It's a fantastic gesture and means so much to us.'

It was perhaps the most honest thing Karen had said in the past ten days.

10

LIFE AT LIDGATE GARDENS

Across Dewsbury and the entire country, children were presenting their mothers with slightly battered bunches of daffodils and brightly coloured cards. It was Mother's Day – the day of the year when children make a fuss of their mums; breakfast in bed, helping with Sunday lunch; boxes of chocolates bought from scraped-together pocket money.

It is a day when mums and their children are supposed to be together. And it seemed even Karen Matthews realised that from the highly emotional appeal she sent out. 'Mother's Day is a day when every mum wants her children around them,' she said. 'I don't want cards or presents, I just want my darling daughter home safely. I know Shannon would normally have made me a Mother's Day card at school and we would have spent the day together.'

If Karen really did know and believe that, it makes her cruelty all the more breathtaking.

She went on, 'I have a special bond with Shannon and I

feel sure that she is alive and will come home to her mum. If you or anyone knows where Shannon is, please think about my family this Mother's Day and bring my beautiful princess home where she belongs with her mum, dad, brothers and little sister.' Then, her face, crumpling into sobs again, she said, 'All I want for Mother's Day is my princess back. We want to be a family again. I'm desperate to hold her.'

Det Con Christine Freeman stood close by as Karen spoke, wiping away her tears. When Karen was finished, Christine went over to comfort her but the tears had already vanished. Again a strange feeling bothered Christine. 'Is it just me or does she only ever cry when she's on camera?' Christine thought.

Meanwhile, just one mile away, Shannon had little idea that it was Mother's Day. Drugged, dazed and often left entirely alone, Shannon had little understanding of what was happening at all. Because, while for the last ten days Karen Matthews' life had been projected outwards by television and newspapers to the entire world, poor Shannon's life had been confined to a couple of smelly, pokey rooms.

Shannon's nightmare had begun that Tuesday afternoon when, still excited from her swimming lesson, everything had suddenly changed. There can be few treats designed to appeal to a young child more than a trip to the funfair – a helter-skelter hurtling through the cold winter air, dodgems crashing into each other, brightly coloured merry-go-rounds and burgers, popcorn, candyfloss and hotdogs.

With the thought of a funfair jaunt already planted in her mind by Karen, that probably explains why Shannon was so quick to jump off the school bus and rush away from her friends that afternoon. Perhaps she had been sworn to secrecy by her mother not to tell any of her friends about the 'special treat' with her 'Uncle' Michael. For Shannon, usually deprived of much fun at home, the promise must have been almost magical.

Michael Donovan had been waiting around a quarter-of-an-hour inside his silver Peugeot 406 car when Shannon ran up to the passenger door and jumped in. 'My mum says you're taking me to the fair tonight,' an excited Shannon giggled, according to Michael's admissions to the police.

'It was right foggy and awful that night,' he went on. 'I don't know exactly why she said that. I drove around Dewsbury and the fog was getting really down.' It was then he came up with his story to Shannon that the fair had been cancelled because of the fog. It was already a bitterly cold late afternoon with visibility cut right down, so Michael's lies must have seemed plausible to trusting Shannon.

Michael then told Shannon that with the weather being so bad they'd have to go straight back to his flat. Shannon was already prepared for the idea. 'My mum said I'll be stopping at your flat,' he claimed she said. But he made no mention of how long Shannon expected to be stopping for or what she expected to find there.

He then drove the unsuspecting schoolgirl to his home in a nondescript row of council maisonettes in Lidgate Gardens, Batley Carr. Once behind the royal-blue front door and away from the prying eyes of neighbours, he led Shannon up the narrow staircase to the group of rooms which would be her entire world for the next 24 days.

The maisonette was reasonably clean and tidy compared with what Shannon had been used to at Moorside Road. The woodwork had been painted a magnolia shade with gold-coloured wallpaper reaching up to waist height. And without the background din of Karen and Craig's constant screaming it must have felt almost peaceful compared to the chaos Shannon was used to experiencing.

In the outside world, thousands of people were searching for her – desperately trying to find some clue as to where she might have gone – but, inside Lidgate Gardens, Shannon was unaware of the hunt, unaware even that she had been abducted. Shannon dashed around the rooms before deciding that, rather than having the bunk beds in the back bedroom where Michael's daughters had once slept, she would have his double bedroom. Michael slept on a bunk bed instead.

That first evening, Shannon sat on a sofa and watched television while Michael prowled nervously around the flat. He claimed Karen had been supposed to ring him at 10.00pm but the appointed hour came and went and there was no call. Karen had no interest in speaking to her daughter, who seemed strangely used to being abandoned on a whim by her feckless mother. Karen finally rang the next day on a phone belonging to Craig's mum and Michael's sister, Alice Meehan.

'She asked, "Is everything all right? Is she settled down?"' Donovan told the court. He told her that she had, but asked why Karen hadn't sent any spare clothes or toys to keep her occupied. Poor Shannon was still wearing the same black school jumper and trousers and Bratz boots from the previous day.

But Karen gave Michael short shrift. 'You've got money – go and buy them,' he claimed she replied.

Even then Karen had no interest in speaking to her daughter. Michael claimed, 'I asked if she wanted to speak to Shannon and she said, "No, I've got to keep it short, stick to the plan, Mike."'

The following days fell into a monotonous routine for Shannon, trapped in her lonely cell with only Michael for company. Together they watched hour after hour of cartoons on television. The pair would eat pizza, takeaways or microwave meals. An example of Michael's desperately low intelligence was that he was unable to even work an oven.

Michael Donovan was widely regarded locally as a 'weirdo' or 'oddball'. He had been born Paul Drake, one of nine children – six girls and three boys – to parents Marian and Joseph Drake. His sister Alice was ten years older than him. According to his siblings, they all enjoyed a largely happy childhood growing up on the Woodsmore estate in Batley where he had been indulged as the baby of the family well into his teens.

He'd shown signs of low intelligence from a very early age – and by adulthood his IQ was just half the national average. Two of his sisters, Jeanette and Maria Harper, described him as a fantasist even in childhood. Michael and Jeanette fought a lot – particularly over their pets – and he worried the entire family by making up outlandish stories and fantasising about being someone else.

By the age of 11, Michael was getting into more serious trouble and it was then he appeared before the juvenile courts on three counts of arson and shoplifting. He was sent to an attendance centre for 12 hours. He was then enrolled at a special school five miles away in Hartshead Moor which was intended to cater for his learning difficulties. But he claimed to be bullied and unhappy there.

At 16, he was convicted of causing criminal damage. Afterwards, he ran away and never returned home. He found work at a tailoring factory, pressing trousers, but the job didn't last long – none ever did – and he then spent brief spells working in a shop, as a labourer and as a delivery driver.

Michael had always been highly impressionable and easily led, but he was also usually the victim of the bullies who led him on then pushed him away. No matter which school, workplace or social group he was with, sooner or later he invariably found himself a target for Mickey-taking which then progressed to cruel jibes and then physical violence.

At the age of 19, fed up with the bullies' taunts about his weedy appearance, his surname Drake and his slow character, he changed his name by deed poll to Michael Donovan, even though he had a brother who was already called Michael. It was the name of an action hero in his favourite science-fiction TV mini-series V. But even calling himself after an action hero – albeit one few people had ever heard of – did nothing to save him from the taunts and jokes of others. Few descriptions of him ever omitted the words 'misfit' or 'oddball'.

As an adult, his IQ was so low he was classified as 'mentally impaired' and had difficulty reading and spelling even the most basic words. Psychologists were astonished that he managed to learn the Highway Code and pass his driving test – even if it did take him more than a hundred lessons before he passed on the second attempt. Driving was the love of Michael's life and he virtually never left Lidgate Gardens except in his car.

An incident recalled by Colin Backhouse, his former

boss at an engineering firm, summed up Michael's stunted intelligence. He had been given a £20 note to fill up the firm's van with diesel but was later seen driving back and forth on the road outside. When asked what he was doing, Michael replied, 'There was only enough room in the tank for £18.40 of fuel, so I drove around a bit so I could use the other £1.60.'

Michael also had a history of mental problems. These were exacerbated in 1991 when, while working as a delivery driver, his pickup truck overturned on the M62 motorway. He suffered serious head injuries and afterwards needed psychiatric counselling. It was during these sessions at a psychiatric hospital that he met his wife-to-be, Susan Bird. It may not have been a terribly auspicious meeting place for the couple but initially they seemed suited and soon after they married.

They went on to have two daughters but the marriage broke up acrimoniously when Susan walked out on Michael in 1998. The split came with claims of abuse being made by both sides. Michael alleged Susan was violent to him, while Susan claimed he regularly beat her up.

It is unclear exactly where the truth lies between Susan and Michael's accounts. But, following the split, a family court judge must have had some sympathy with his case, because he was awarded custody of the couple's daughters. Michael was clearly devoted to his girls but was simply unable to cope with growing children and their constant needs. Within a short time, neighbours noticed that the girls appeared neglected and unkempt. When they started school they often turned up clearly not having been washed or their clothes cleaned. Some neighbours even sent round spare clothes for them to wear.

The home was dirty and gave off a smell of neglect. Michael rarely let anyone into the family home and also tried to prevent his daughters from leaving whenever possible. As the girls grew up, he banned them from playing out in the street with other local kids. Instead, they would be seen looking out forlornly from their bedroom windows as other children messed around in the street below. The girls grew up timid and shy, barely able to make eye contact with strangers – very like little Shannon.

After years of concern, the girls' school called in Social Services. Michael said he'd tried to look after them 'as best I could' and the family was closely monitored. But social workers became increasingly worried about the girls' welfare at Lidgate Gardens.

Finally, they were taken into care. Social workers were worried that by then the elder girl was looking after both her father and younger sister. There had also been a worrying incident when a teacher found a love letter from Michael to one of his daughters in her lunchbox. Around the same time Michael was involved in a road accident and needed a long period of hospital treatment. Even if he still wanted to look after his children, he was no longer capable of it and they were taken away.

Soon after the girls were put into care, police returned to Michael's home and took away a computer, video recorder and dozens of videos. It was only when the girls were away. from him and safe that it emerged their father had become increasingly bizarre and weirdly controlling as the years had passed. It was claimed had tried to order their lives through a succession of self-adhesive notes covered in rules which were stuck around the house. These were chilling precursors of the rules written up for Shannon which were to dominate her own time at Lidgate Gardens.

One neighbour, Ann Kitchen, later recalled being asked to babysit the girls when Michael was out. 'It was the strangest thing I have ever seen,' said Ann, 58. 'The poor children were scared stiff to do anything because of dozens of rules stuck all over the flat.

'There were ones on the fridge and cupboards, saying, "Do not open". There was another on the phone, saying, "Do not answer".

'There were others on the walls, saying things like "Dad's room, do not enter" and "Do not talk". Can you imagine banning your children from talking? It was very odd. I tried to make conversation with them but they said they weren't allowed to talk. The phone rang so I asked the eldest, "Are you going to answer it?" But I was told only their dad was allowed to answer the phone.

'I asked if they wanted a drink but they said no one was allowed into the kitchen apart from their dad. These house rules weren't just a daft joke. He obviously imposed them very strictly.'

Another neighbour, Hayley Brown, 24, described Michael as 'a real weirdo'. 'He had these big, scary eyes and was really spooky,' she said. 'The kind of bloke you wouldn't want to bump into on a dark night. One time he got locked up overnight because he had tampered with his meter to get free gas. He kicked off with the gas people and the police were called.

'I took his kids in for the night. When I cooked a meal for my boyfriend, they walked over to his plate and just started grabbing food off it with their bare hands. When it was time for bed, I gave them a quilt to sleep under but they didn't want it. Instead, they used their coats as blankets. Both of them put the coats over their heads to sleep. It was really weird.'

Michael was allowed access visits to his daughters after they had gone into care but for him that was not enough. He launched a legal battle to get them back permanently. But, when that bid failed in 2006, a more sinister side to his character became apparent. It had been agreed he could collect his elder daughter for an access visit one afternoon after school. But, rather than return her to her foster parents at the appointed time, Michael went on the run with her to Blackpool in breach of a court order.

There he checked into a bed and breakfast under false names and stayed for three days before being tracked down by the police. He was charged with abduction but when he appeared at Bolton Crown Court the prosecution offered no evidence and the case was dropped.

However, the entire relationship with his daughters and the Blackpool 'abduction' showed that, despite Michael coming across as little more than an 'oddball' to neighbours, he was actually quite capable of well-thought-out and controlling behaviour when it suited him. Michael had also had another more recent run-in with police when he accepted police cautions for attempting to obtain property by deception. The property had been medicine.

By the time Shannon was abducted, Michael was on a wide range of daily medication including anti-depressants and tablets for dystonia – a neurological condition which caused muscles in his legs to spasm and tremble. He was also taking Temazepam to help him sleep at night.

Even in court Michael was described as an 'inadequate' and only just able to get by amid the complications of the

modern world. His appearance did little to help his image
as an oddball. His face was gaunt with cheeks hollowed
out from having lost all his teeth. His hair was cropped
short and his eyes could appear staring and crazed. The
waxy pale skin on his face only added to the impression he
was in bad health, worsened by a dreadful diet consisting
almost solely of microwave chips and potato waffles, fried
eggs, mushrooms and lager.

Since his road accident he had walked with a limp. And
on bad days his dystonia could make him very unsteady
and likely to fall over. He had seemingly given up all hope
of working again and settled down to a life on benefits. All
in all, he cut a rather pathetic figure shuffling around
Batley Carr. He spent most of his time shut in his
maisonette, only venturing out to visit family, collect his
benefits or to buy food and lager. The only other time he
was spotted outside his flat was to wash or polish the
beloved S-reg Peugeot 406 he had bought for £2,500 a few
months before Shannon's abduction.

He was treated as a 'dimwit' figure of fun at most places
that he went. And he would certainly never have given the
impression of a criminal mastermind able to keep one step
ahead of hundreds of police officers from across West
Yorkshire for more than three weeks.

As Karen Matthews got to know Michael after that first
meeting at Brian Meehan's wake, he must have appeared
the perfect co-conspirator for her wicked plan: a convicted
criminal who could be easily led, with access to sedative
drugs and who lived alone just far enough – but not too far
– from Dewsbury Moor and with his own means of
transport. He even had form for abducting a child.

One of the few people who took the trouble to speak to

Michael was June Batley who lived in the flat below him. The pair would share occasional chats over mugs of coffee, but she had little idea about the true nature of her strange neighbour. And when she didn't see him much during that February and early March she assumed he must have a new girlfriend who was keeping him occupied.

When she later heard a child's footsteps up above, she thought they must be those of the girlfriend's child. 'We heard tiny footsteps which we thought was a toddler, not a nine-year-old. No way,' she later recalled. June only heard noise and footsteps on about three occasions, which considering Shannon was held prisoner there for 24 days is remarkably little. Most likely this is because during her incarceration there she was usually sedated and probably rarely moved around the flat at all.

As the days passed by at Lidgate Gardens, Shannon was fed a foul combination of drugs including the sedative Temazepam, the adult painkiller Tramadol, another painkiller Dihydrocodeine, the anti-depressant Amitriptyline and Traveleeze travel-sickness tablets. Four of the drugs discovered in her system were prescribed to Michael and the other – the travel-sickness tablets – was available over the counter. The effects of the mix of so many drugs would have left Shannon sleepy for most of the time and lethargic and confused when she was awake.

During her hours of consciousness, Michael was careful to ensure she never switched over from cartoons to the news where she might have learned about the hunt going on all around her. At other times he would keep her occupied by letting her play Super Mario computer games and music on the CD player.

On top of the large television sat a list of handwritten

rules on a sheet of A4 paper ripped from an exercise book. The rules shaped every moment of Shannon's existence while at Lidgate Gardens – just as similar rules had once shaped the lives of Michael's daughters.

Under an underlined title 'Rules' was written:
   * You must not go near the windows
   * You must not make any noise and bang your feet
   * You must not do anything without me being there
   * You must keep the TV volume low – up to
     volume eight
   * You can play Super Mario games and some DVDs
     and you can play the CD music.

The list ended with the large thick initials: 'I.P.U.' Detectives later discovered that IPU was Karen's coded threat for Shannon, standing for 'I Promise You'. In the corner of the sheet of paper, Shannon had drawn a pink Bratz symbol – a poignant reminder of the age and innocence of the girl being incarcerated under such a cruel regime.

At one end of Michael's flat, hanging from a loft hatch hung a long, elasticated white strap which had been hoisted over a beam in the roof space. The end hanging downwards had been tied to create a noose.

At first, Shannon must have wondered what the contraption was for – but when Michael first prepared to go out and leave her alone in the flat she was to discover its horrific purpose. Using the noose, she was tied up like an animal, leaving her just enough movement to use the toilet and watch television, but with no chance of escape. Each time Michael went out, usually into Dewsbury to buy food or medical supplies, Shannon would be tethered with the noose and told not to disobey the list of rules under any circumstances.

It's not thought Shannon was ever physically abused during her time at Lidgate Gardens. But question marks still hang over what she may have witnessed during this period – and how psychologically damaging it may have been. After her release, detectives found several drawing by Shannon including one in which she had sketched a penis with a hand around it. Below were written the words: 'Mummy and Mike'.

Yet, in Michael's warped thinking, he believed Shannon's period of captivity was one of enjoyment for her. 'During the time Shannon was with me we stayed mostly in the house, although sometimes I would go out and buy clothes, food, toys, games and DVDs,' he later told the police. 'She said I was kind and generous, not like her parents.'

Taking Shannon out of the flat was a massive risk for Michael, considering the scale of the search going on all around. But the stress and boredom of being stuck inside day after day must have made him feel it was a risk worth taking. And so, on at least three occasions, he sneaked her into the back of his car when no neighbours were around and drove away.

Once, just as dusk was falling, he drove her to a Tesco supermarket at Batley. Another time he took her to the Asda store in Dewsbury. Both times Shannon sat in the back of his car, her pink hood pulled up to cover her face, while Michael did his shopping. CCTV footage discovered later showed Michael calmly wandering the supermarkets like any other shopper, seemingly without a care in the world and without any sign that the nation's most wanted child was sitting outside in the back of his car.

So relaxed was he in one shop that he even stopped to put coins in a charity box on his way out. On three other occasions, Michael took Shannon to parks in Batley and Birstall and on another evening he just took her for a ride in his car to 'give her a break from the house and get some fresh air'.

It had been many years since Shannon's own mother had bothered to take her out on a trip to a park and in some perverse way perhaps Shannon's jailer was being kinder to her than Karen ever had. In fact, one of the first sounds that alerted Michael's downstairs neighbour June Batley to the fact that a girl was in his house was the sound of laughter – something that had rarely been heard at 24 Moorside Road.

Day after monotonous day passed by in the stuffy, stifling atmosphere of Lidgate Gardens, with little to break the boredom. As the search outside ground on amid a growing sense of hopelessness, little Shannon was again sitting quietly, unnoticed and uncared for, playing quietly on her Super Mario and watching cartoons.

11

'I CAN'T TRUST ANYONE'

In the second week after Shannon's disappearance, life in Dewsbury Moor picked up a routine, which, although very different from the norm, soon became accepted by the locals as the way things were now. Police officers kitted out in high-visibility jackets were dotted all over Dewsbury Moor and the buzz of the police helicopter came and went overhead.

Specialist body-search dogs were fussed over by locals as they sat waiting to start their shifts. Twenty-seven of the dogs had been drafted in from Greater Manchester Police for their skill in searching for the scent of bodies which could have lain dead for weeks. Coincidentally, the same kind of specially trained spaniel dogs were also being used at another huge investigation just under way at that time in a former children's home on the island of Jersey, where there had been allegations of child cruelty and killings.

The press were still out in full force too, their cars parked up and down Moorside Road together with TV and radio outside-broadcast units. Meanwhile, the Community House retained a buzz of activity as meetings were held, posters designed and endless piles of leaflets printed and delivered. Fundraising for the campaign had also been successful with football clubs including Huddersfield Town, Leeds United and Bradford City donating shirts and other memorabilia for auctions and raffles. Local rugby teams including Bradford Bulls and Leeds Rhinos also stepped in to help.

With the police forensic investigation of their home complete, Karen and Craig were back living at 24 Moorside Road, but, even if Karen appeared utterly unmoved by the absence of her daughter, it was having a devastating effect on the rest of the family. Each night Shannon's two-year-old sister went to bed cuddling her missing big sister's favourite teddy. In the morning she woke up crying out for Shannon who had previously always been lying in the bunk above her. Being so young, she was largely unaware of the huge search going on for her sister; she simply missed the playmate who had also acted as a surrogate mother for her when Karen couldn't be bothered.

Even Shannon's older brother had forgotten about the usual sibling squabbles they'd had and was now desperately missing her. The excitement for both of Shannon's brothers at finding themselves centre stage in a major drama had worn off. Now the reality of life without the sister they'd teased yet quietly loved was starting to sink in.

Even the family's pet dog, Scania, was pining for Shannon as she mooched around the house whimpering and sniffing at her toys and clothes. Shannon had doted on Scania who had been a gift from Craig's mum Alice. The mongrel had then been named by Craig after an advert for cut-price supermarket Netto which carried the slogan 'Scandinavian for Value'.

'Shannon loves that dog,' Karen told reporters. 'You can see Scania knows she is missing; she won't keep still and she normally lies under the table and not move [sic]. She is walking around looking for something.'

Karen and Craig continued to spend much of their days at the Community House. Craig showed an interest in the searches and leaflet campaigns but Karen preferred chatting to her mates and was constantly darting to the door for a cigarette outside. Her mood seemed relaxed away from the reporters and cameras and, while many of the volunteers at the Community House were impressed by her apparent bravery in such a crisis, others who popped in and out felt uneasy at the way she seemed to be able to laugh and joke so carelessly.

Back home, behind closed doors, Karen's life had returned pretty much to normal. She returned home one afternoon carrying a crate of Carling lager. And Craig was frequently sent out through the press pack to the local 'offy' for supplies of fags and booze – one day staggering back with 48 cans of beer.

While Craig always kept his mobile phone in his hand, as though constantly waiting for the call to say Shannon had been found, Karen seemed strangely calm most of the time. She had slipped back effortlessly into her routine of drinking, smoking and watching telly – although more often than not it was now her daughter who was occupying the news channels.

One of her more bizarre outbursts of behaviour was when she was visited by local *Yorkshire Evening Post* reporter Richard Edwards. He had been following the story and built up a good relationship with Karen and Craig. But one day when he knocked on the door and it was opened, he stepped into the hall to find it deserted. Finally, from behind the living-room door leaped Karen, yelling 'boo' and tickling him in the ribs. 'What on earth was going on?' Richard Edwards recalled thinking to himself. What, indeed?

Sometimes Karen would flick through the cards and letters from well-wishers which were now arriving from around the country – and even elsewhere in Europe. The police had been impressed by the raw emotion of Karen's Mother's Day appeal and were keen to use her again. The West Yorkshire Police Press Office realised that Karen, like Kate McCann, might prove to be their most valuable tool in keeping the case at the top of the news agenda.

And so on 3 March – Day 13 of the search – Karen was back in front of the media again for one print and one television interview, to be pooled to any other media organisation that wanted it. Karen was flanked by Shannon's headteacher Krystyna Piatkowski in a show of support. This time Karen's eyes were bloodshot from crying when she sat down in front of the TV crew. Tears were soon welling in her eyes before a solitary drop tipped over her lower lashes then dribbled down her face.

In Karen's hand, she held the teddy which she claimed Shannon had adored. But, if she was being honest about how much Shannon loved the little teddy and used it for reassurance, then it is hard to fathom the cruelty of depriving her of it, knowing she was to be in such unusual and disturbing circumstances away from home and all things familiar for so long.

Karen pursed her lips and breathed deeply in an attempt to hold in her sobs as she told the interviewers that she still couldn't bear to go into Shannon's bedroom and was crying herself to sleep every night. Then she went on to defend herself against claims Shannon must have been unhappy at home to have written the message on her bedroom wall about wanting to live with her father.

She simply put that down to Shannon 'having a bad day'. 'She's not the child to go running away,' Karen insisted. 'I can't understand the reason why she would say things like that because nothing has ever made her do it before.'

Instead, Karen painted a picture of domestic bliss at 24 Moorside Road, claiming Shannon's last words to her mum as she skipped off to school that Tuesday morning were: 'See you at teatime, Mum, I love you.'

Recalling that poignant moment, more tears flooded down her pale cheeks before rolling on to the neck of her baggy white sweatshirt. As the interview went on, Karen spoke about the police checks that were taking place into every member of her family. She accepted them as an inevitable part of the investigation, but she let slip something which instantly sparked interest among the news teams analysing the footage.

'The family don't feel safe any more – it has broken the family apart,' said Karen. 'It makes me think I can't trust the people who are really close to me any more.'

What on earth could Karen mean by that? Was she referring to Craig? As stepdad in the chaotic family situation, he'd been regarded as a suspect by a lot of people following the case.

Reporters wondered if Karen had some inkling as to

who had taken Shannon and she was trying to get the message out. Another theory was that the police had coaxed her to say the words in the hope of scaring and flushing out Shannon's abductor. Whatever the motive, Karen's words had one very clear result – they totally deflected any suspicion from herself in the public's mind. Whether this was all part of Karen's masterplan is difficult to tell.

But she had quickly learned how to manipulate the press. The anguish in her face at the end of that public appeal made brilliant TV footage. Her direct appeal to any abductor was heartbreaking. 'If you have Shannon, will you please let her go,' she pleaded.

After Karen's interview, Leon Rose also spoke about how he was coping almost a fortnight on. Clearly still suffering shock as well as confusion and loss, he seemed unable to fathom what might have happened to his daughter. 'I have no idea,' he said quietly. 'All I know is that she went to go home from school and didn't go home. That's basically all I know.'

The following day marked the second week since Shannon's disappearance. For all those locals who thought she'd be home by bedtime that first afternoon she went missing, it was a difficult milestone. But again the people of Dewsbury Moor came out in a show of togetherness and solidarity with Karen and Craig.

More than a hundred people – many still wearing their Shannon T-shirts – turned out just before 6.00pm on another cold evening for a vigil to remember the missing girl and to pray for her safe return. The mood was more downbeat than the previous week when some shred of hope had still remained. This time, Karen, dressed in her familiar green parka jacket, and Craig, in his ever-present Rockport baseball cap, stood at the front group of well-wishers, Karen holding the hand of Shannon's friend Megan.

Karen was apparently too distraught to speak and just nodded at friends and neighbours in the crowd, before bending down to light a candle for Shannon. Then other youngsters came forward from the group and lit dozens of red and white tea lights laid on the ground in front of the Community House.

When all the candles were alight, the flames spelled out the word Shannon – a message of hope which was broadcast on television sets across the country that night. More balloons were released bearing messages of hope, and then local vicar Kathy Robertson spoke to the crowd, saying, 'We wanted to come and share our love and support for the family, as Shannon's memory is so much in our hearts and in our minds.'

Then the group sang 'He's Got the Whole World in His Hands', changing the words to 'He's Got Shannon and Her Family in His Hands' before a poem called 'Missing' was read aloud and Westlife's song 'Home' was performed by a singer and accordion player. 'We are marking the second week of Shannon's disappearance and coming together as a community to bring our love to what can only be described as a very dark situation,' Canon Kevin Partington said sombrely.

It was indeed dark but the police remained committed to finding Shannon no matter what the cost in manpower and resources. Media commentators were blasting the tabloid newspapers for only being interested when middle-class kids went missing and the police were adamant no such accusations would be flung at them.

More than 250 officers and 60 detectives remained committed to the hunt, either searching further and further afield, tracking down family members and friends, or checking on the homes of registered sex offenders in the area. A full DNA profile of Shannon had also been created by experts using swabs taken from her family and fingerprints from her school books.

It was then announced that another 3,000 homes in the Dewsbury area would be searched and their occupiers questioned, in addition to the 300 flats and houses which had already been covered. Det Supt Andy Brennan was desperate to keep up the pressure on whoever might be holding Shannon. Meanwhile, his press officers were trying to drip-feed information from the case to retain public interest, and details were released about Shannon's pink tankini swimming costume and stripy blue towel with its fish motifs.

Karen and Craig then permitted the public a closer view of their grief when they agreed to allow a reporter and cameraman from the *Yorkshire Evening Post* into their home, up the shabby stairs, past the scruffy sign announcing 'Shannon Room: Keep Out', and into the little pink-and-blue bedroom which had been her refuge.

Karen had obviously tidied up for her visitors and even put new bedding on Shannon's top bunk, apparently bought especially for her homecoming. It was the shot every news organisation had been desperate for – the room from which little Shannon had been missing for 15 days. Her porcelain dolls were still lined up on the windowsill, Bratz toys sitting on top of the wardrobe and her Dalmatians-print dressing gown hanging on the edge of the bed, as if she had just tossed it there moments earlier.

Karen claimed she had barely entered the room since Shannon's disappearance (even though her younger daughter was still sleeping there). 'It has seemed so empty since she has been gone I haven't been able to come in,' said Karen. 'This has been the longest I have been in here since she went missing.'

Posing for a photograph by the girls' bunk beds, Craig seemed keener to chat than Karen. He was anxious to emphasise how good his relationship with Shannon had always been. 'Me and Shannon have always got on well, we have a real good laugh together,' he said. 'She likes jumping on me and trying to beat me up.'

Then he went on to talk about how he was also still dealing with the shock and grief of his father's death four months earlier and his aunt's death two months before. Pausing to control his emotions, he said, 'I am trying to be strong for Karen, it is hard for all of us. I don't think I've got my head around losing my dad yet, so we are all trying to keep each other going.'

Karen was adamant Craig was the strong partner in the relationship though. 'He has been a rock for me,' she said. But she claimed the worry and exhaustion was a huge burden. 'Wherever I am the stress is always there,' she said. 'I toss and turn at night, I can't sleep properly. We think she is out there somewhere and that she is going to come home. It is that thought that keeps us going.'

The next day there was another opportunity for the public to get even closer to the story and share Karen's pain – just as they had done the previous summer with the McCanns. This time it was the release of a recording of Karen's 999 call to police, made just before 7.00pm on Tuesday, 19 February.

It was fascinating listening for the millions who tuned in to the TV and radio news that evening. To all the telephone operator's questions, Karen immediately had an answer – yes, she'd already looked everywhere she could think of; yes, she had checked with all her schoolfriends; no, Shannon had never done anything like this before; and no, there was just nowhere else she could look.

As the conversation went on, Karen's voice appeared to crack as she apparently took in the full horror of her daughter's disappearance. It was a superb performance, with deep gulps and attempts to control her breathing in a bid to hold back tears. Even Karen was pleased with her performance. When she heard the message being aired again during a news report on TV while sitting with reporters, she clutched Craig's hand as if in need of support. Then tears again welled and fell when her younger daughter pointed to the picture of Karen on the TV screen and said, 'Mummy.'

'It is hard to hear it again,' Karen murmured. 'But anything that makes people think, anything that helps get Shannon home, is worth it.'

Some of Karen's friends then came up with the idea of consulting psychics to see if they could help find Shannon. Karen, Craig and Amanda Hyett saw three different mediums privately after Shannon disappeared, although gradually the story leaked out.

All three of the psychics assured Karen that Shannon was alive and well. In reality, of course, they were absolutely right but at the time they were dismissed as giving false hope to a desperately troubled mother.

During one of the meetings, Karen claimed the psychic told her of a flat in Dewsbury where Shannon could be found. The following morning, Karen reported the meeting to detectives, giving them directions to the supposed flat where Shannon was being held. Keen to pursue every possible avenue, two detectives were immediately dispatched to the property but after talking to the occupier it was soon clear Shannon had never been there. It was another blind alley.

But at another meeting between a psychic, Karen and Craig, at a neighbour's house in Moorside Road, her plan was almost exposed. 'She was taken by someone you both know. She is alive,' the medium said. Then, slowly turning to Karen, she added, 'You know where Shannon is.'

Karen began to cry – her normal escape route in times of trouble – but others in the room recalled she looked terrified. Friends tried to console Karen who claimed she was now frightened because the psychic must mean that she was familiar with the abductor and the place where Shannon was being held. By doing so, she deflected attention from what the psychic might really have meant – that she knew the actual place where Shannon was at that exact moment.

Karen then asked if Shannon was being hurt by her abductor but the medium was insistent that she wasn't. Egged on by her friends, Karen was forced to hand over a tape of the hour-long meeting to detectives. The accuracy of the psychic sessions must have chilled Karen – did she fear that they might even have revealed her as the abductor too?

Perhaps from fear of what the psychics might reveal next, Karen played down her visits when asked about them. 'Yes, a few of us did go to see a psychic but I wasn't listening to everything and taking much notice of everything that was said,' she said when news leaked out about the trips. 'I do and don't believe in what they have got to say. I'm not sure.'

But Karen was more than happy to send officers off on a wild goose chase to the address mentioned by one of the psychics. It proved another welcome distraction from attention focusing on herself. On another occasion she also told officers she was worried about a man who had been sitting outside her home in a car. Valuable police man hours were spent investigating the sighting before the man was identified as a loan collector. He was traced and eliminated from the inquiry.

As the hunt continued, a JCB digger was brought in to help shift wasteland opposite Crow Nest Park, close to Shannon's home. The land was covered with thick undergrowth, uprooted trees, rubble and fly-tipped waste and the digger was needed to force through large tracts of scrub. Officers armed with garden forks and spades then followed on behind carefully sifting through the uprooted soil, smashed vodka and beer bottles, dumped furniture and general trash for any scraps of clothing or belongings that might have been Shannon's.

Hundreds of bits of material and clothes had been retrieved during the search and dozens of them were presented to Karen and Craig by their family liaison officers for identification, but each was rejected as not belonging to Shannon.

On Friday, 7 March, the police issued a new picture of Shannon taken six months earlier at the start of the new school term at Westmoor Junior. Shannon looked more cheerful in this picture, with a wider smile on her slightly chubby face. Her fringe still bore the hallmarks of a 'home cut' but she was neatly turned out. It served as a chilling reminder of how much had changed for the little girl in such a short space of time.

Det Supt Andy Brennan again appealed for help from the public. 'We want people to think back to the afternoon of Tuesday, February 19th when Shannon was last seen,' he said. 'Were you picking up your own children from school that afternoon or were you travelling in and around Church Lane close to Heckmondwike Road? Did you see Shannon?' He then asked people to think of any family members, partners, friends or neighbours who had been acting oddly since Shannon's disappearance.

Detectives hoped briefly they might have one potential breakthrough when two schoolboys came forward, saying they thought they had seen Shannon, alone and sobbing, late on the afternoon that she had disappeared. One of the boys said, 'She was crying her eyes out. There were tears running down her face. I didn't say anything to her. She had no coat on. But her plastic bag was full so it was probably in there.'

Karen reacted predictably to the new sighting: 'It breaks my heart to think she was so upset and we didn't know why,' she said. 'Why did no one comfort her and bring her home?'

The boys' alleged sighting of Shannon alone and unhappy lent weight to the idea that she had become very down after being targeted by a gang of school bullies.

Then, in another interview, Megan told how Shannon – her 'bestest friend' – had been victimised for a number of weeks by other girls calling her 'fatty, ugly and stupid' before kicking her. Megan said Shannon had told her she sometimes used to go away and hide in a secret tree house but she didn't explain where and police were never able to locate such a place.

Sadly, little Megan said, 'I sat on the bench at school today on my own at break time, because I'd no one to play with. Shannon's chair at school is empty and I've no one to sit next to now. I just want her back. She was the bestest friend in the world. I liked everything about her. She was kind and, if I wanted to play with a toy she was playing with, she'd let me join in. She made me laugh and we'd talk about our Bratz dolls because we really love them.'

The picture painted of Shannon was becoming clearer and yet more tragic – that of a timid little girl, sad at home and bullied at school. The reality was probably not very different – except worse, for her mother and supposed protector was in fact her greatest betrayer.

12

DOUBTS START
TO GROW

For more than two weeks there had been nothing but
sympathy for Karen Matthews right across Britain.
Privately, people might have questioned her morals – so
many kids by so many men – and her parenting skills, as
well as the message Shannon had scrawled on her bedroom
wall. But in print and on television there was nothing but
empathy for Karen and her terrible plight.

But then, gradually, the mood started to change. No one
quite knew where the rumours started but gradually it
emerged that all was not as rosy behind the closed doors of
24 Moorside Road as Karen and Craig had portrayed. And
there was a growing sense that the odd-looking stepfather
might have something to hide. His gormless, geeky look
with a baseball cap invariably pulled down over a blank
expression and gaping jaw did nothing to help his case.
Nor did his lingering body odour and his obsession with
spending hours alone on his computer every day – even at
the height of the search for Shannon.

After Shannon had been missing a fortnight, rumours about Craig and his temper gained ground. The tabloid newspapers went out of their way to rubbish the gossip. But of course such coverage only served to transmit the local gossip to a national audience.

Then, on Friday, 7 March, during an interview with *GMTV*, Karen Matthews took on the snipers and gossip-mongers directly. She said there was no way Craig was involved. 'I know it has nothing to do with him,' she said. 'He would not hurt anybody. It is very hurtful to think people think he would do something like this, because he would not.'

She then told of the comfort he had given her over the past few weeks. 'I cry, he cuddles me,' she said. 'When he cries, I cuddle him. We try to just comfort each other.'

Karen's starring appearance on *GMTV* – one of her favourite daytime-TV shows – must have been hugely exciting for her.

As she was being interviewed, the contrast between perfectly highlighted and designer-dressed reporter Elaine Wilcox and Karen Matthews could not have been greater. Karen and Craig were wearing their oversized 'Find Shannon' T-shirts on top of their ordinary clothes as they sat and talked to the camera at the Community House.

'I think something sinister has happened but I'm convinced that she is still alive,' Karen said. 'Yeh, I know she is,' she reiterated. And at this point a smirk seemed to creep across her face.

Investigative psychologist Prof David Canter, who later analysed Karen's television interviews and appeals, concluded she was clearly 'getting a kick out of pulling the wool over the eyes of the public and local community'.

Again, in footage for the show taken at the Community House, Karen was filmed walking to camera seemingly unable to control a grin forming. The TV crew put Karen's strange behaviour down to nerves. Little could they know she was actually having a private laugh at the expense of Fiona Phillips, Kate Garraway and all the highly paid *GMTV* sofa celebrities whom she had watched a million times from her own sofa in Dewsbury Moor.

The barely discernible smirks were repeated in other bits of footage of Karen taken during Shannon's disappearance. Prof Canter concluded they were caused by Karen's sense of embarrassment at everything going on around her – an embarrassment which someone engaged in the real emotion of the disappearance would never, ever feel.

Karen's defiant support for Craig on *GMTV* actually only served to fuel doubts in some viewers' minds about the fish-counter worker. Could Karen have realised this? And, if so, was she hoping to indirectly frame him for the abduction when, in fact, it was her own work? Karen's vocal defence of Craig also had the effect of provoking her parents to come out with their version of what life was really like inside 24 Moorside Road.

It was Day 19 of the search – Sunday, 9 March – when the true state of Karen Matthews's family life began tumbling out in an interview Gordon and June Matthews gave to the *Sunday Mirror*. They told how they had repeatedly tried to persuade Karen to leave Craig in the weeks leading up to Shannon's disappearance amid a string of bust-ups.

June was clearly struggling to cope with not having done more to save the little girl she called her 'Little Miss Smiley-Face'. 'We used to see her a lot,' June said, thinking back on her happy memories with little Shannon. 'She'd come round for tea. She would peer in through the front-room window. She is a lovely, happy girl. I just want to see her little smiley face at my window again.'

Gordon was so angry that Karen's feckless lifestyle had ultimately resulted in his granddaughter disappearing off the face of the earth that he said he could no longer have anything to do with Karen or Craig. 'I now consider them to be completely disowned and I want nothing more to do with them,' he said. 'If my daughter is going to turn a blind eye to what he is like, then that goes for her, too.'

It was certainly a strange reaction, considering it was still possible Shannon had been abducted by a total stranger and Karen was wholly innocent of any crime. Then Karen's brother entered the fray, revealing for the first time Shannon's desperate state when she had turned up at his house the night before her disappearance, begging not to be sent home. And he told about the bruises he'd seen on her body in the past.

Craig immediately went on the offensive against the claims being made against him. He branded Martin's accusations 'b***sh*t' and rubbished his Karen's mother's allegations. 'I thought June would say that,' said Craig. 'Karen's mum wants to rule Karen's life. I've been with Karen for four years now. I have never hit her or any of the children. We play about as you do, but me and Karen have a brilliant relationship. I was working on the night before she went missing so I don't know if she came home upset.

'I work stupid hours a day so I couldn't do it anyway and I wouldn't. Loads of people will tell you that I won't do it. There is no point. I love those kids. I know they're not mine but I treat them like they are.

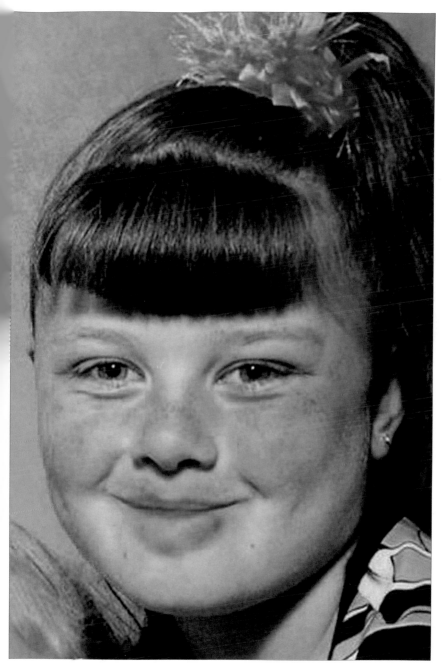

Innocent Shannon Matthews, who suffered a terrifying ordeal at the hands of her own mother.

© Rex Features

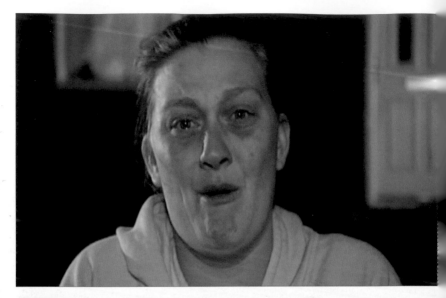

Mother from hell. Karen Matthews, who deceived the nation into thinking that her daughter was missing. She posed with Shannon's favourite teddy and made tearful television appeals for the return of her child.

Karen poses for the press on her doorstep with boyfriend Craig Meehan.

Above: CCTV footage showing Shannon shortly before she disappeared.

Below left: Members of the Police Underwater Search Unit search a storm drain during the hunt for Shannon.

Below right: Door-to-door enquiries. The hunt for Shannon cost in the region of £3.2 million.

The community of Dewsbury Moor rallied around Karen Matthews and went out of their way to help in the search for Shannon. The local children even helped her plant flowers for the missing girl.   © *PA Photos*

Some noticed how Karen Matthews seemed to carry on with her
normal life, even though her daughter was still missing.   © *PA Photos*

She didn't turn up at home and that's why I started getting worried, she hadn't turned up.

Above: Shannon's former home, now boarded up. © PA Photos

Below: Karen Matthews being interviewed by the police. © Rex Features

Above: A computer reconstruction showing how Michael Donovan was hidden with Shannon Matthews in the base of a double bed when police turned up at his house.
© *Rex Features*

Below left: Michael Donovan, who was found guilty of kidnapping Shannon.
© *Rex Features*

Below right: How the *Daily Star* reported Karen Matthews being brought in for questioning again by the police.
© *Rex Features*

'June is lying because she doesn't like me. She wants to tell Karen what she can and can't do. There is only me who works. I bring money into the home. I feed them. They get everything. My money goes on Karen, bills and the kids.'

There were others who backed Craig too. Karen's cousin Susan Howgate, described him as 'kindest, gentlest person' who 'loves kids and would never, ever hurt anyone'. Karen was, apparently, 'a brilliant mum and loves her children 100 per cent'. And Dewsbury Moor neighbour Petra Jamieson seemed to hint that it was Craig who took on the burden of parenting in the house. 'Craig keeps himself to himself. He makes sure the kids have been fed and put to bed, and makes sure they go to school on time.'

Even Leon Rose showed his support saying his daughter had never complained to him about Craig and that he found him to be a 'decent bloke'. 'They got on really well,' he said. 'I was not around for some years and he [Craig] has been a real dad to her.'

Karen remained stalwartly loyal to her partner – or so it appeared – dismissing her family's allegations as 'rubbish' and saying Shannon loved her stepfather. 'It has broken my family apart,' Karen said, talking about Shannon's disappearance and the family fall-out which had followed. 'It makes me think I can't trust the people who are really close to me any more. Her brother's crying. Her sister's crying. Half the time I cry myself to sleep. Her step-dad Craig cries himself to sleep.'

Such were the allegations being flung around Dewsbury that finally the police had to ask family members not to say anything further about each other publicly for fear it might hamper the investigation.

Showing a quiet dignity in contrast to the abuse being

batted backwards and forwards among the Matthews and Meehan families stood Leon Rose. He may have only had limited contact with his daughter over the past year but since her disappearance he had dedicated his every spare moment to the search. On Monday, 10 March – Day 20 of the search – he agreed to take part in another press conference in a bid to keep the story 'live'.

He told reporters he now feared Shannon was being held captive. 'Terrible though that thought is, in some ways that gives me a strange sort of hope,' he said. 'At least she would still be alive and there would be a chance that she might be released unharmed.' Then, in a direct plea to any kidnapper, he added, 'She's a good lass, she hasn't done anything wrong. I'm sure she wants to go home. Friends and family are missing her. This nightmare needs to end. I beg anyone who may be holding Shannon – please, please let her go free.'

Leon said his personal search would not stop until Shannon was back home. 'I can't bear the thought that we don't know where she is,' he said. 'Every morning I wake up hoping: "Could this be the day we find her?" But the pain goes on. I feel so empty when I go to bed knowing she is still out there and we haven't found her.'

In a press conference called in Crow Nest Park, Chief Inspector Graham Armitage said, 'This is the biggest investigation of its kind now, it's certainly the biggest missing-persons inquiry since the Yorkshire Ripper which I also worked on.' The mere words 'Yorkshire Ripper' sent the press into a frenzy and the police press office had to emphasise Chief Insp Armitage had been talking about the scale of the inquiry rather than its nature, as Shannon was still being treated as a missing child not a murder victim.

Despite that, more than half of the UK's 'cadaver' search dogs, specialising in looking for dead bodies, were working on the case, brought in from as far away as Hampshire and Strathclyde. Dog handlers were working 14-hour days to maintain the intensity of the search, backed up by other officers still searching homes and businesses in the area.

And there was still a huge amount to be done – police were still just two-thirds of the way through a list of 3,000 residential and commercial premises. They had searched dozens of homes of the 300 people they had managed to identify on a family tree for Karen and Craig.

The searches even included June and Gordon Matthews' home. For four nights, the elderly couple had to move in with June's sister while their house was turned upside down in the search for any clue that might bring them closer to Shannon. Gordon was outraged when he was questioned about a blanket discarded in the cellar of his home.

'I had a blanket in a dustbin in the cellar, I keep it there to cover the carpets when we decorate,' he recalled. 'They opened it and asked me if she was in the dustbin. I said, "You're pathetic, I would never hurt her, I adored Shannon." But we were treated like suspects, her own grandparents. It was disgusting.'

But, of course, officers were more concerned with finding Shannon than preserving people's feelings and the searches continued to rampage across Dewsbury.

On Tuesday, 11 March, Shannon had been missing for exactly three weeks. The bitterly cold days and nights at the start of the search had softened to the beginnings of spring and there was even a hint of sunlight some mornings as officers set off on their duties around Dewsbury Moor. But there wasn't a single ray of light in the search itself.

To mark the third week, locals from the Moor organised a sponsored walk to remember her and to raise much needed funds for the 'Search for Shannon' campaign. It was just before dusk at around 6.00pm when dozens of friends and neighbours gathered outside the Community House for the third consecutive week. They hadn't been standing there long when the heavens opened and they were lashed with rain, as if to compound the gloom of the mood around.

After a few minutes, the rain eased off and the group then began another slow walk towards Shannon's home with Karen, Craig and Leon united again, standing side by side. At Moorside Road, children signed a specially made card intended as a gift for Shannon 'when she comes home'. They were determined that on her return Shannon would see that she had never been forgotten by anyone on the estate. Parents helped toddlers unable to write to make handprints on the card.

But, despite gargantuan efforts, even the locals' campaign appeared to be running out of steam, with fewer people turning out for the leaflet drops and poster blitzes on the towns around Dewsbury. 'There were over a hundred of us at first,' said Dawn Battle, who lived nearby and was a classroom assistant at Shannon's school. 'But as time goes on people have their own lives to deal with. But we have to keep on trying to get out to as many places as possible, because it just might make the difference in finding her. I helped Shannon with her reading for about 12 weeks and from being a really quiet girl she really opened up and we got on great. I feel like this is the least I can do to help.'

Then, in a last-ditch attempt to flush out any information about Shannon's whereabouts, the *Sun* suddenly more than doubled its reward to £50,00. Finally the target figure Karen had been hoping for had been reached.

But what would happen now? Was it time for her and Michael to move into the second phase of their plan and release the girl just where he would then be able to 'discover' her in Dewsbury Market? Karen was probably too busy to even consider it, with the number of appeals and press interviews she was doing.

The following morning, she and Craig appeared live on Radio 4's *Today* programme in a slot normally reserved for politicians or leading business people. During the interview, Karen reaffirmed her belief that her daughter had been abducted. But this wasn't a friendly local newspaper reporter Karen was up against and interviewer Sarah Montague, more used to tackling media-trained cabinet ministers, wanted to know *why* Karen thought Shannon had been taken by someone she knew.

'It seems that way because there's no trace of her at all,' said Karen. 'There's no trace of her swimming costume, her towel or anything like that that she's taken with her.'

Asked why someone Karen knew would take Shannon, she answered, 'Just to hurt me, really.' And as to who might have taken Shannon, she could only reply, 'No idea at all. All my friends and family have all been checked and there are no sightings of her things there at all.'

But Karen knew full well that not *all* her and Craig's extended family had been checked – because no one had ever even mentioned the existence of Michael Donovan to them yet. The interviewer then went on to probe the allegations. The interviewer repeatedly returned to the number of children Karen had produced by different fathers. By the end of the show, a massive furore had erupted about the nature of the interview and the repeated questioning about the number of kids Karen had.

Many listeners were outraged – that a traumatised mother should be quizzed on her family set-up at such a difficult time. Writing in the *Guardian*, Beatrix Campbell said Karen had been 'subjected to an interrogation that appeared to position the mother as the perpetrator. Has any other apparently blameless mother been so sweetly assailed?'

Again there was much debate about why Karen and Shannon were being treated so very differently in the media to Kate and Madeleine McCann. The well-meaning *Independent* newspaper blamed the double standards on class. 'Kate and Gerry McCann had a lot: they were a couple of nice middle-class doctors on holiday in an upmarket resort … Karen Matthews is not as elegant, nor as eloquent.'

But the paper's attempt at highlighting social injustice was lost on Karen who told a Channel 4 documentary crew, 'They say it is because I'm not high class, innit, like that McCanns family and I don't make an effort, put make-up on and stuff like that. It is disgusting comparing a council person to a snob.'

Even the *Brisbane Times* on the other side of the world used the case for a dig at the British class system, claiming that Karen Matthews and Kate McCann represented the two sides of the social-class coin in Britain. And the *Daily Telegraph* said, if Shannon had been from a middle-class family with articulate parents capable of launching a slick public-awareness campaign, she would have received far more attention in the press.

But, for all the pontificating of the broadsheet

newspapers, in reality it was still the tabloid papers that kept the story alive and the *Sun* which had put up a reward, although the tabloids' stories were increasingly casting doubt on the domestic set-up of Karen and Craig.

Even after offering its reward, the *Sun* suggested Shannon might have run away because she didn't get on with Craig. Karen was furious. 'I think it's sick,' she said. 'They give a reward and then they put that.'

But the concerns about Karen and Craig just could not be shifted from people's minds. Det Con Christine Freeman was certainly becoming increasingly uneasy about the pair. When 27 new victim-recovery dogs were added to the search, she tried to break the news gently to Karen that these creatures would be looking for a body. She was stunned by the response.

'Hmm,' Karen said. 'Take me to the post office to cash my giro?'

Christine also felt uneasy about the amount of time Karen spent poring over the story in the Sun that it had upped its reward to £50,000. After an entire career spent working closely with victims of crime, Karen's behaviour was the most unusual Christine had ever come across. Nagging concerns which had been bothering the officers dealing most closely with Karen and Craig for more than three weeks were now turning into alarm bells. But with not a shred of evidence or clue as to Shannon's whereabouts, the waiting just went on.

13

DISCOVERY

Disco music was pumping from the DJ stand at Staincliffe Cricket Club just up the road from Dewsbury Moor. Karen and Craig were stood in a corner quietly chatting. Around the room were all the other locals who had played such a huge part in the search for Shannon over the past three weeks.

The 13 March disco had been arranged by community stalwart Julie Bushby to give everyone the chance to let off a bit of steam – and to raise money for the severely depleted 'Search for Shannon' fund. It was roundly agreed to have been a good night and, as locals went home, some a little worse for wear, they couldn't have dared hope that the end of Shannon's captivity was now just hours away. Except, that this time, it was.

Unbeknown to the party-goers at the cricket club – including Karen herself – earlier in the day Michael Donovan had been talking to another relative about the search for Shannon. The relative told Michael that the police were compiling a family tree for Craig and Karen and would want his details included in it so he could be eliminated from the inquiry.

But Michael – neither intelligent nor cunning – flatly told the relative he didn't want his details passed on. Naturally, it rang alarm bells and within hours his reaction had been reported to the police. So that evening, as the people of Dewsbury Moor danced to Abba and Take That, Michael was being catapulted into the position of the police's 18th most 'significant individual' suspect.

What made him particularly of interest was that Alice Meehan, Amanda Hyett, Craig and Karen had never even mentioned his name. More than 350 names had been entered on a family tree branching out from Karen, Craig and the fathers of her children. But his wasn't one of them. That became all the more surprising when a quick criminal-records check on his name threw up the case against him for abducting his daughter which had then been dropped at court.

Next morning, rumours were circulating around the estate that Craig had taken an overdose following the disco. It was never established whether it had been a serious attempt, a cry for help or indeed a total fiction which had been passed around from neighbour to neighbour. But interest in the story was soon overwhelmed by the extraordinary events about to unfold.

It was mid-morning when Detective Constables Nick Townsend and Paul Kettlewell were dispatched to Michael's flat in Lidgate Gardens, Batley Carr, to interview him. Batley Carr is just a mile northeast of Dewsbury Moor, but, separated by the A638 Halifax Road, it felt like a distant place to many of the locals of Dewsbury Moor who rarely ventured far from home.

But from the windy top of Dewsbury Moor, Karen Matthews would have been almost able to look down dimly into the distance towards the flat where her daughter was being imprisoned. Batley Carr is essentially one large council estate built originally as a home for mill workers. It had suffered with the collapse of manufacturing industry and ensuing unemployment but, with a population of less than 4,000, most of the residents knew each other and there was a strong sense of community centred around its pubs and working men's club.

It was still overcast yet feeling warmer that Friday lunchtime when the two detectives turned up at the front door of Michael Donovan's maisonette at the foot of a steep bank. The first daffodils were making an appearance in neighbouring gardens and it really did feel as though, after one of the hardest winters in memory, spring had finally arrived.

The two detective constables had carried out an incredible 700 'actions' – phone calls, interviews or door-knocks – in the 24 days that Shannon had been missing. And, like hundreds of their colleagues in the West Yorkshire Police, they were now facing the grim reality that the little girl would not be found alive.

The pair were both nearing the ends of their careers, with more than 60 years' service between them. Det Con Kettlewell, sharply dressed and a stickler for standards and detail, was approaching 55 and due to retire in just six months' time. Det Con Townsend was almost 49 and due to pick up his pension after 30 years in the force. But, although perhaps more old-fashioned in their techniques than some of their younger colleagues, they knew the value of patience and dogged determination in an inquiry like this – or 'old-fashioned bobbying', as they liked to call it.

The two thick-set men, both with strong Yorkshire accents, had also seen enough heartbreak in their careers to be committed to doing anything they could to save a missing little girl. But, as they banged on Donovan's front door at about a quarter to one that lunchtime, there was nothing to indicate this interview would be any more fruitful than any of the others they had carried out over the past three weeks.

After a couple of minutes, it was clear no one was answering the door. Rather than retreat to their car, the pair walked round to the back of the maisonette and tried knocking again. Still no answer. But Kettlewell and Townsend were the kind of coppers unwilling to be easily put off and knew the answer so often lay in a bit of local knowledge. It was then that they started knocking on doors of neighbours.

'He must be in, he never goes anywhere without his car,' said one neighbour pointing at the silver Peugeot 406 still parked by the kerb in Lidgate Gardens.

The suspicions of the two policemen were pricked further. Their next call was at the home of Michael's downstairs neighbour, June Batley.

At first, all she could offer was that she thought she'd heard Michael's footsteps overhead earlier in the day. But on further questioning she revealed something truly astonishing. She told how over the last few weeks she had heard a child's footsteps in the flat above too, although she'd assumed it must be the daughter of Michael's new girlfriend.

'I think it was my chief constable who later described the overall investigation as like trying to do a jigsaw without the benefit of the full picture to refer to,' Det Con Townsend later recalled. 'At that moment in time, June Batley had just handed us the box lid.'

The pair instantly realised the seriousness of the situation and called for back-up from the force's search team, the Operational Support Unit based in Wakefield. Thirty-five minutes after first knocking on the door, the detectives were joined by PCs Ian Mosley, Matthew Troake and Peter Greenwood.

The group carried a battering ram and were no strangers to piling through suspects' front doors at any time of the day or night. They held a brief discussion on the doorstep as to how best to tackle the situation. If it was the wrong house and an innocent person's door was smashed down for no reason, there would be no end of paperwork and apologies to be dealt with. But it was a risk worth taking.

At 1.20pm, with a huge crash, the uniformed officers smashed down the front door then straight through an interior door into the hallway. Det Con Kettlewell was first in, pushing himself into the hallway. There was no time to think what might greet him at the other side or whether a panicky and desperate abductor might be armed or dangerous.

Followed by his colleagues, Kettlewell sprinted up the narrow stairs to Michael's living area. There he paused for a moment trying to hear if he could make out any noises in the flat. It was totally silent. At that moment he thought June Batley must have been mistaken about the sound of footsteps and Michael must have gone out.

Nevertheless, the policemen continued to search the flat in the hope of finding any clue to Shannon's existence. It was then that the uniformed officers found another locked door – which led to Michael's bedroom. Again, they had to use force to break open the door, storming into the bedroom, which also seemed deserted.

PC Ian Mosley could smell cigarette smoke as soon as the door caved in and he felt sure it had been recently occupied. He leaned across and put the palm of his hand on the sheet of the double bed in the centre of the room – it was warm. In the hallway Det Con Kettlewell was just walking towards the bedroom to join his colleagues when he heard the words which sent a chill through his heart.

'Stop it, you're frightening me,' a child was saying.

But, weirdly, the voice seemed to be coming from inside the bed. Detective Constables Kettlewell and Townsend exchanged a look of confusion. Meanwhile, PCs Mosley and Greenwood moved closer to the side of the bed and slowly started to lift it. The bed felt unusually heavy and it was at that point children's clothes started spilling from a hole underneath it.

Then everyone's attention turned to the shuffling noise on the other side of the bed. And there, from the tiniest hole, the small figure of a child squeezed herself head first on to the carpet. She was bedraggled, with tousled brown hair, her face pale with fear and with tears running down her cheeks. But there was no doubting who it was.

Shannon was alive.

PC Greenwood leaned down and helped pick up the girl who was slumped in a pile on the floor. His colleagues watched in shock as she steadied herself on her feet and looked around the room staring at the officers squeezed into the bedroom.

Slowly, PC Greenwood guided the girl across the room towards Det Con Kettlewell. And then she said the words everyone had waited so long to hear: 'I'm Shannon.'

Det Con Kettlewell, a father-of-three himself, bent down and, with the air of a man well used to sweeping children to safety, he lifted up the tearful girl and carried her securely downstairs and towards the daylight.

'Where's Michael?' he asked, desperately trying not to frighten the girl further.

But the answer was matter-of-fact. 'Mike's where I was,' Shannon replied. 'He's under the bed.'

Neighbours had already gathered outside 26 Lidgate Gardens, alerted by the smashing of the front door. There were gasps of shock as the little girl emerged in Det Con Kettlewell's arms. 'Is it Shannon?' one neighbour asked quietly as she was carried to the waiting police car.

'Yes,' replied Det Con Kettlewell. 'She's OK.'

It felt like at that moment the whole of Batley Carr gasped in shock. Then, with Shannon safely ensconced on the back seat of the car, Det Con Kettlewell pulled out his mobile phone and called in the news to his superiors.

Back inside the upstairs room, the remaining officers had soon found Michael in his hiding place. With Shannon safely out of the room, PC Matthew Troake had peered into the hole from where the child had escaped and was confronted by the hollow-faced visage of Michael Donovan. He was still curled up in the foetal position inside the divan, even then apparently unable to realise that the wicked plot hatched in the Dewsbury Moor café was over.

'Come out of there,' PC Troake shouted into the bedframe. But Michael carried on lying perfectly still as if he couldn't hear a thing. Troake yelled his command again but still Michael refused to budge. Even when he was formally arrested on suspicion of abduction, he lay utterly motionless.

PC Troake and one of his colleagues then lifted up the bed and began pulling Michael out from underneath it. He had created a secret compartment by removing the drawers and sliding himself and Shannon inside it. Next to him were a packet of Traveleeze tablets, a prescription for Temazepam and, somewhat ironically, a copy of the *Sun* announcing the reward for Shannon's discovery.

At that moment, Michael would have known it was all over – there never would be a reward or fame. Just a lengthy jail sentence and national loathing awaited him. As the reality began to dawn, Michael started to fight the officers surrounding him like a man possessed. He lashed out, kicking, swearing, biting and shouting as they tried to handcuff him and pull him out of the room.

Michael later claimed that officers were rough with him, banging his head against the floor, kneeling on his thigh and shouting, 'Now we've got you, you bastard.' But PC Mosley vigorously denied the claims in court. Instead, the court heard how Michael had continued to resist being taken away even as four officers tried to carry him down the narrow staircase. All the way to the front door Michael continued fighting and flailing his body around, smashing his hand on the landing wall in the process.

Outside his front door, Michael was oblivious to the small gathering of onlookers, dragging his feet on the ground, refusing to be carried to the waiting police car. Neighbour Christopher Heaps, who lived just doors away, recalled, 'I heard the commotion and looked out to find out what was going on. I saw this bloke walk down the steps carrying this girl in his arms. I asked, "Is that Shannon?" and he said, "Yes." She looked absolutely fine. She looked as if she had been well cared for. She was clean and tidy, her hair was brushed and her clothes were clean. She was calm, but very very quiet. Then I saw the police drag a man out of the flat on his knees down the steps. He was handcuffed, he did not want to go with them.'

Another neighbour, Mandy Dixon, 33, said Michael made one last bid for sympathy as he was dragged away. 'People were shouting at him. He turned round and said back to us, "Don't hate me – I'm a poorly man."'

Michael was lifted to the police van, shoved inside and the door slammed firmly behind him.

As the noise of the closing door echoed around Lidgate Gardens, the officers stood still, exchanging glances of disbelief, barely able to take in the enormity of what had just happened. The mammoth inquiry which had cost £3.2 million and used 10 per cent of the entire's force's manpower was over. And Shannon was alive. She was safe.

'It was the most surreal moment of my life,' PC Greenwood said later. 'I'm a father myself, so the recovery of that little girl, having been on the case for two or three weeks … it was an emotional time.'

With Shannon sitting safely strapped in the back of the detectives' police car, Det Con Townsend and Kettlewell slumped into their seats in the front. The pair both turned and smiled at the fragile child sitting behind them, then stared at each other. As they were big bluff Yorkshiremen, there was no backslapping or hugs as you might see in American cop shows, just one hand stretched out across the gearstick, grabbed by the other and shaken warmly.

But there was no doubting the tide of emotion sweeping through the two men. Looking back, Det Con Townsend likened the experience to that of the births of his children.

'We looked at one another and I've got to say the emotion began to well up,' he recalled. 'Paul was already glassy-eyed. I looked over the seat at little Shannon in the back seat sitting on a load of exhibit bags, I looked at Paul and I cried tears of joy. Simple as that.'

Det Con Kettlewell referred to it as a 'defining moment' of his career. 'I felt very privileged to be one of the two officers who located her. For 24 days, we thought that Shannon was dead and I think most of the colleagues I spoke to who were on the investigation team were of the same mind as me. It was an emotional rollercoaster, it really was. I carried the little girl out and I couldn't believe that I was carrying Shannon.

'In the police car me and Nick shook hands. We were euphoric. We had a little girl in the back seat who didn't appear to have a clue as to what was going on and two upset burly policemen sat in the front of the car. She must have wondered, "What's it all about?"'

Det Supt Andy Brennan was with his deputy, Det Chief Insp John Gilbody, when he received a phone call on his mobile telling him Shannon had been found. At first he misunderstood the message and thought he was being told that a body had been found. By this stage almost everyone on the inquiry was considering it a murder investigation.

But when the caller explained that there was no body and Shannon was actually alive and well, Det Supt Brennan insisted the message be repeated again – he literally couldn't believe what he was hearing.

Detective Constables Townsend and Kettlewell drove Shannon to Dewsbury Police Station – the scene of where so many messages and appeals for information about her had been broadcast over the past three weeks. There she was guided into a quiet room and handed a colouring book and pencils. Finally she was free, free to be a carefree little girl, safe and secure.

14

'GET KAREN
DOWN HERE'

Michael Donovan was bouncing around in the back of the police van on his way to Halifax Police Station when he uttered the words which gave the investigation an even more bizarre new twist. 'Get Karen down here, we've got a plan,' he said. 'We're sharing the money – £50,000.'

His words hung in the air for a few seconds before officers in the van began a flurry of calls to senior officers waiting to question Donovan at Halifax Police Station. Could Karen really be in on it or was Michael simply lying to shift blame from himself and point the finger at Shannon's poorly educated and feckless mother?

Back at Lidgate Gardens, a full search had immediately swung into action. One of the first things that was found on top of the television was the A4 page entitled 'Rules' which had cruelly dictated Shannon's life for the past 24 days. As the search of the flat continued, one of the officers punched open the loft hatch to make one of the most shocking discoveries at the scene.

There he found the white elasticated rope tied to one of the roof beams which had been used to tether Shannon when Michael had to leave her alone and go out for supplies. Equally disturbing were two packed bags in the bedroom and over £600 in cash Michael was carrying in his pocket. It led detectives to believe that, with the net closing around him, Michael had been on the verge of bundling Shannon into the back of his car and quitting the area. They believed Michael had been thinking of fleeing to Blackpool again – just as he had done with his elder daughter less than two years earlier.

Amid the mess and old papers turned up in the search was a colourful, childlike drawing of Blackpool Tower. There seemed no other reason why Shannon would have drawn that picture unless Michael had mentioned visiting Blackpool. Detectives believed that Shannon's fringe had been recently trimmed, as if to disguise her, and that Michael had recently bought a 'child on board' sticker for his car – both factors adding weight to the Blackpool theory.

Despite his hapless appearance, it seemed Michael was more than capable of planning and carrying out quite detailed plans when he needed to. 'It's my belief that, had Donovan taken the opportunity and escaped on the day Shannon was rescued, I don't believe that we would have recovered her alive,' said Det Supt Andy Brennan.

Det Con Kettlewell is also horribly aware that things might have turned out differently had it not been for his and Det Con Townsend's persistence. 'I like to think it was down to mine and Nick's old-fashioned bobbying that led to the result,' he recalled. 'It would have been so easy to walk away and think, "Well, we'll visit Mr Donovan on another day."'

Within hours, a large section of Lidgate Gardens had been sealed off, with officers posted all along a length of plastic tape barring entry into the flats and maisonettes. A white tent was erected over the front of the house inside which Michael's front door hung off its hinges. Scene-of-crime officers, in white paper suits to prevent contamination of evidence, came and went for the rest of the afternoon and evening carrying out a thorough forensic search, testing for fibres, fingerprints and DNA samples which would provide the vital evidence for when the case came to trial. And later, Michael's prized Peugeot 406 was also taken away for examination.

Michael was booked in at Halifax Police Station at 2.25pm. Wearing a white shirt and black trousers, he seemed to be struggling even to walk across the custody suite and had to be held up by two officers. Once in the interview room, he suddenly became far more reticent than he had been in the police van, refusing to answer any questions, and he made no further reference to Karen and the reward.

Later, however, after consultation with a lawyer, he prepared a statement of his version of events in which he described the meeting in the Dewsbury café and how Karen had initially asked him to look after one of her sons. 'She then asked me to take care of Shannon and again said there would be money in it for me,' the statement said, adding that, when Michael appeared unwilling to cooperate, Karen threatened to 'get three lads on to me'.

'I know one of the people she mentioned had stabbed a man and killed him,' he said in the statement. 'I was frightened if I didn't do it they'd come after me.' But Michael never supplied officers with names for these men.

Then he claimed he reluctantly told Karen, 'OK, I'll do it,' and she then gave him the sheet of paper with his instructions for the abduction.

His statement went on to explain how the following day his car was broken into and a sat-nav device stolen from the glove compartment, and, when he was next visiting Alice Meehan at Dewsbury Moor, Karen had flagged down his car and said to him, 'I see you've got your window fixed.' When he asked how she knew about the window, he claimed she replied, 'Remember the plan or else they will come and burn your car out.'

Michael claimed that by then he was so terrified of Karen he had to go along with her plan. The statement then went on to describe the night he went and picked up Shannon, who believed she was being taken to the fair. When he was back at his home, he learned about the search for Shannon from the television.

'When I saw the news, I wanted to take her back home but I was still frightened of Karen's threats to set men on me if I did,' the statement said. He went on to describe how he had taken Shannon on trips in his car during her time in captivity and even claimed that Shannon had described him as 'kind and generous' because he'd bought her clothes, pens, crayons, a Bratz doll and even a badminton set while she was with him.

He claimed Shannon had told him how different he was to her parents who were always rowing and how Craig had once thrown a can of lager at her head. The 'bombshell' element of Michael Donovan's statement, however, was the claim that, in the second week of the hunt for Shannon, Karen had called him to discuss the reward. 'She said it had gone up to £30,000. I thought from the news it was 25. She told me if it went up to £50,000 she would ring me and I would know what to do.'

At around the same time as Michael was being hauled off to Halifax Police Station, Karen Matthews received the news she claimed to have been anticipating for 24 days – that Shannon had been found alive and well. In reality, it must have struck a chill into her heart. The game was up.

Neighbour Peter Brown – Natalie Brown's husband – was the first person in Dewsbury Moor to hear Shannon had been found. 'I got a call off a very good source that she was safe,' he recalled. 'I went straight round to Karen's, it was about 2.00pm. Karen and Craig were sitting there, hoping for good news. I said to Karen, "Don't quote me on this, but she has been found." Karen just looked so shocked, she froze, then she broke down in tears, Craig was the same.'

There were no screams of joy, no demands for explanation or confirmation from Karen. Just silent shock. It was only much later that Peter understood exactly why she must have been so stunned.

Peter himself didn't stop shaking for hours. 'It was an amazing feeling, the best feeling ever,' he said.

In the next few minutes, more reports of Shannon's release began to arrive. Natalie Brown received a text message saying people in Dewsbury's Asda Superstore were saying Shannon had been found. Within a couple of minutes, text messages and phone calls were flying in all directions. People were even sending instant messages on MSN saying the hunt was over.

Karen and Craig sat stunned, almost motionless in the eye of a storm, as excited and emotional locals who had worked so hard to find Shannon whirred around them.

Within minutes, a police car was outside Moorside Avenue and Det Con Mark Cruddace and Con Alex Grummitt had joined the neighbours squashed into the house, which was already buzzing with excitement. The officers asked the friends to give them a couple of minutes alone with Craig and Karen.

Karen sat hunched on her squashy black leather sofa staring at the officers intently. Next to her sat Craig, even his usual gormless expression lit with interest. Face-to-face with the couple, Det Con Grummitt confirmed the rumours which had been swirling around the Moor. When he had finished speaking, the pair looked at each other and hugged. Then Karen turned away so the officers couldn't see her face. 'It was a very unusual reaction,' Det Con Grummitt recalled. 'Craig's eyes filled up and he appeared very emotional. Karen didn't ask any questions like, "Where have you found her?"'

Of the millions of questions that would have been hurtling around the mind of any other mother whose daughter had been missing for almost four weeks, none seemed to be bothering Karen Matthews. A list of questions which should have been torturing Karen for the past 24 days ought now to have been tumbling out: Had Shannon been hurt or abused? Was she upset? Had she been fed? Who had taken her? Where had she been kept? Did she know she was being searched for?

But Karen didn't ask a single thing – not even if her daughter was OK. Instead, Karen got a few things together and prepared to be driven to Dewsbury Police Station where she was told Shannon had been taken. Throughout the 20-minute drive, Karen still barely revealed a flicker of interest in her missing daughter's welfare. In fact, the only thing that provoked a reaction during the entire journey was when Det Con Grummitt's mobile-phone ringtone played a snippet from the hit song 'Crazy' by Gnarls Barkley.

'I like that ringtone, you must text or send it to me,' Karen shouted from the back seat.

Det Con Grummitt was stunned. 'I thought, "We've just found your daughter and you ask about the ringtone,"' he recalled. 'In my opinion, it just wasn't right.'

It had been decided to keep Shannon at Dewsbury Police Station 12 miles away from her abductor Michael Donovan at Halifax, for security and to prevent any cross-contamination of evidence or witnesses. Within an hour of her arrival, everyone within the station was treating her like a celebrity. Officers and admin staff took any excuse they could find to peek through a window at the little girl quietly doing her colouring in. They could barely believe this was really her – this was Shannon.

One of the first people to greet Shannon at Dewsbury Police Station was Det Con Christine Freeman, Karen and Craig's family liaison officer. She had been halfway through interviewing someone else when a colleague interrupted her with the news that Shannon had been found. She, too, initially assumed they must mean a body. But the broad smile on her colleague's face disclosed that, against all the odds, there could be a happy ending to what had been a terrible saga.

'She was under a bed in a flat. She was with a man called Michael Donovan, Craig's uncle,' the other officer said.

The words immediately sent a shiver through Det Con Freeman. She had spent literally hundreds of hours with Karen and Craig since Shannon's disappearance – but not once had they mentioned an uncle with the name Michael Donovan. And if not, why not?

Det Con Freeman sped back to the police station where she found Shannon still busy colouring, oblivious to the celebrations breaking out all around her. 'Am I glad to see you,' Freeman said, smiling at the quiet youngster, who was seemingly bemused by the amount of interest in her.

'Are you?' she replied quietly.

Christine sat down next to Shannon, desperate to wrap her arms around her and hug away all the fear and uncertainty she must have felt over the past 24 days. But she couldn't – any physical contact with Shannon was banned until all the forensic examinations had been completed. So, instead, Det Con Freeman made do with giving the little girl a comforting smile.

After a while, Shannon stood up and wandered around the room, as if trying to make sense of her new surroundings after so long spent incarcerated in the same few rooms. She walked to a window and frowned as she saw the row of cameras out the front of the police station, their long lenses all pointing in her direction. News that Shannon had been found safe and well had leaked out, and the world's press – even those that had lost all interest in recent days – were back in force in Dewsbury.

'What's that?' Shannon asked pointing to a television news crew.

'Nothing,' Det Con Freeman replied, uncertain how to tell the shy nine-year-old that she was now one of the most famous faces in the country.

Det Con Freeman was then briefed on what Michael had claimed about Karen in the back of the police van. Deep down she wasn't even that shocked. It just confirmed what she had increasingly suspected over the last few days. But suspicion was not enough – proof was what was needed if Karen was to be convicted.

As Karen arrived at Dewsbury Police Station at around 2.30pm, she looked pale and tired but devoid of any real emotion. Next to her, as usual, was Craig. Det Con Freeman met her colleagues Alex Grummitt and Det Con Mark Cruddace and together they guided Karen and Craig to the room where she would finally be able to see Shannon again.

Christine's expression remained as fixed as Karen's own, hiding her sense of disgust as it became increasingly apparent what Karen had done. Inside the small room, Karen stood in front of a window looking into the room next door. But all Shannon could see in the other room was a mirror, having no idea she was being watched through it. This was the nearest Karen was going to get to Shannon for quite some time.

Det Con Christine Freeman explained to Karen that she couldn't hug or touch or even talk to Shannon until all the forensic tests has been completed. Experts would need to analyse all fibres found on Shannon's clothes in the hope it would reveal where she had been and who she had been with. Touching others could lead to cross-contamination, so they had to remain apart. But in reality that was just part of the issue. If Karen really had been in on the plot, there was no way they could let her near her daughter and run the risk of her threatening or coaching her to stay quiet. But, on the other hand, eventually she had to be allowed to see her daughter. What if Donovan's claims were fantasy and Karen was wholly innocent?

But Karen's behaviour in the next couple of minutes utterly convinced Christine that there was nothing innocent about Shannon's mother. As Karen stood in front of the window looking at her daughter, there wasn't a hint of emotion. 'She's got new clothes,' Karen finally blurted out in her flat, expressionless tone. And that was it. There were no tears of joy or relief. No questions as to how she had been or where she had been found. And no demands to be able to hold and cuddle her daughter after such a painful separation.

Afterwards, Christine Freeman said, 'If it were me, I'd have virtually been breaking the glass down to hug her.' But not Karen. Instead, she turned and silently left the room. Det Con Mark Cruddace recalled seeing tears well up in Karen's eyes after seeing Shannon. But who could tell if they were tears of joy or tears of despair that her plot had failed.

Karen and Craig were taken straight to a discreet hotel away from Dewsbury Moor where they would spend the night. Having been through such a roller coaster of emotions in recent days, it wasn't felt appropriate for them to return home to the media circus outside their home and the well-meaning if frenetic band of supporters inside it. While they were away, Karen's other three kids were cared for by her friend Petra Jamieson, leaving her and Craig alone that night to consider what would happen next.

The news Shannon had been found safe and well was also quickly communicated to her father, Leon Rose. He described the moment of learning the nightmare was over as being 'like winning the Lottery'. 'I'm over the moon,' he said. 'I thank everyone that helped. I said before I wouldn't give up. I'm just thankful she is home.'

Craig's sister Amanda Hyett had helped Karen get into the police car to go to Dewsbury Police Station to see Shannon. She was visibly moved by the news. 'I can't believe it – what an incredible relief,' she gushed to reporters.

Her husband Neil was in Barnsley on a coach-driving job when the news broke. 'My wife rang me, she had heard something but she wasn't sure at first,' recalled Neil. 'Then I started to get some more messages and we realised it was true. She had been found and she was safe. All I wanted was to give her the biggest cuddle ever. Craig had been so strong all the way through but I saw him start to get upset on Thursday night. Now he can celebrate getting that little girl back.'

Shannon's friend Megan Aldridge was equally ecstatic. 'I want to see her now and give her a big hug,' she said. 'I'm so happy because I have been really missing her.'

At the girls' school news shot around the classes that Shannon was alive. Girls screamed and cried as they hugged each other. Headteacher Krystyna Piatkowski told how she, the staff and pupils were all 'delighted and relieved' that their missing classmate had been found.

There were celebrations too at the police incident room where officers had worked 14-hour shifts, collating information and checking statements. 'Everyone was in tears,' Det Supt Andy Brennan later recalled. 'I've never seen an incident room like it. It was a very emotional time. The vast majority of staff and officers were parents or grandparents themselves. They didn't need anyone to remind them of the consequences of not finding Shannon.'

At the Community House, a large cheer ripped through the building as the good news was confirmed over the telephone to Julie Bushby. Local people who had toiled night and day in freezing cold conditions had almost ceased to hope there could be a happy conclusion to their efforts. But, with the news that Shannon was safe, tears fell and friends and neighbours hugged and squeezed each other until they were short of breath.

'This is absolutely brilliant news,' said Julie Bushby. 'We are all delighted to hear it. The main thing now is getting Shannon back with Craig and Karen where she belongs and helping that family get back to normal.'

But it wasn't to be quite that simple. Within hours of Shannon's rescue, she had been made the subject of an Emergency Police Protection Order and it was revealed that in the short term she would be cared for by Social Services. Initially, the order was to last for 72 hours but it could be extended beyond that.

With Michael Donovan having made the claim about Karen's involvement, there was no way police could return Shannon to her mother. But nor could they tell Karen or the media and the public the real reasons why. Instead, the news was broken to Karen that it was simply 'procedure' while Shannon was interviewed and underwent medical tests for any physical or sexual abuse. Karen meekly accepted the order and its reasons. She made no demands to be instantly reunited with her daughter, to hold her or to even send her a message through police officers.

It must have penetrated even Karen Matthews' super-thick skin that the game was up. Shannon and Michael were both free to talk to police now, and could she dare to hope that both would not mention her involvement? It was highly unlikely. The general public were still unaware of Karen Matthews' involvement, though, and the last thing the West Yorkshire Police needed was an even greater media circus around Karen – just as they were trying to flush out the truth.

So a carefully worded statement was released to the press, a painstaking attempt to assure everyone that keeping mother and daughter apart yet further was perfectly normal – despite a traumatic abduction which had lasted almost four weeks. 'As part of our ongoing enquiries, and following medical checks, West Yorkshire Police will begin the process of interviewing Shannon,' the statement read. 'This may be a long process but throughout this inquiry our main focus has been, and continues to be, Shannon's welfare.

'We have therefore taken the decision that, for now, it is in Shannon's best interests that she be made subject of an Emergency Police Protection Order. This will remain in place until we have had time to establish the full facts of what happened in the time since her disappearance.'

The idea was also planted in the public's mind that Shannon might be away from home for quite some time to come – perhaps up to three weeks – as the interviewing process would be extremely lengthy.

During questioning, everything Shannon said would have to be filmed on video to save her giving evidence when the case went to trial. And strict guidelines on interviewing children meant she could only be questioned by someone skilled at talking to vulnerable children to ensure the experience was as untraumatic as possible. It was going to be a long, slow process.

Meanwhile, police sources were telling trusted reporters that Shannon would not be allowed home until they were '100 per cent certain' that no one else in her family was involved in her abduction.

Back at Dewsbury Moor, scenes of unrestrained joy had broken out. A sense of raw delight that Shannon had been found safe and well was bursting from every home and resident.

While Karen and Craig were at the police station to see Shannon, their house filled up with family, friends and well-wishers from all over the estate. There was standing room only in the living room and others squeezed into the shabby kitchen where, by mid-afternoon, cans of lager and fizzy wine were being popped open in swift succession. Shouts of 'We'll be having a party tonight' boomed out of open windows towards the gathering press teams outside.

As more and more locals heard the news and flocked to Karen's house, the party spilled out on to her front patch of grass and then on to the other side of the green metal fence. Within a couple of hours, it seemed the entire road was a swaying mass of smiling, drinking, hugging and singing people, all euphoric that a dream many had ceased to believe in had actually come true.

As the celebrations continued, messages of support and congratulations flooded in from far and near. The Mayor of Kirklees Jean Calvert's sense of 'immense relief' was echoed by Conservative Party leader David Cameron who spoke of his 'huge relief on behalf of Shannon and her family'. The Rector of Dewsbury, The Rev Canon Kevin Partington, said it was what the church had been praying for.

'When there is an outcome like this,' he said, 'it really is an answer to our prayers. We hope that this wonderful news about Shannon is going to give hope to other families that may be going through a similar torment.'

Surely he must have been referring in part to Kate and Gerry McCann, whose search for their daughter had now entered its tenth month. When news of Shannon's release broke, they were among the first to send out a message of support. They said they were 'delighted' Shannon had been found alive and the news gave them 'great hope'.

The couple's spokesman Clarence Mitchell went on to say, 'Suffice to say that they will keep on looking until they have a happy resolution in Madeleine's case. It proves that children can go missing for whatever reason and still be found alive. They will keep on looking as long as there is hope.'

How hurtful it must have been for the McCanns when they later discovered that they too had been tricked into sympathising with Karen Matthews.

As dusk turned to dark, the party in Dewsbury Moor was getting into full swing. Someone dug out some fireworks left over from the previous 5 November and let them off in the street. And, as the bonfire-night bangers and sparklers flashed through the gathering dusk, the people of Dewsbury Moor couldn't have yelled and screamed with delight more had they been at the world's largest pyrotechnics display.

Further up the street, another neighbour had found a half-empty tin of paint and written the words 'Welcome Home' on an old bedsheet and hung it from a window. Someone else dug out a small bank of disco lights and hooked it up to an extension lead. Soon shots of neon light were piercing out into the night sky as pounding house music blasted from a set of speakers.

Clutching cans of John Smith's bitter and Asda lager, wine bottles and even litre bottles of Coke mixed with spirits, neighbours drank and danced in the street outside Karen's home. There was a line of people out the door at the corner shop as residents queued up to replenish the quickly depleted supplies of alcohol.

Newspaper photographers and camera crews were in the thick of the celebrations, snapping away as the swigging and singing intensified all night. One local supermarket offered revellers free champagne and the corks popped for hours. When it ran out, someone apparently called up and asked for more.

Friends of Karen hugged each other as they spoke of their joy. Vicky Saunders, 29, a cousin, said, 'I was jumping up and down when I heard the news. I thought, "Yes yes, I can sleep tonight – I haven't slept for ages."'

Neighbour Dawn Battle described it as finally waking up after a very bad nightmare. Some of the revellers confessed openly that they had given up hoping Shannon would be found alive, which made their joy all the greater.

As the night wore on, someone brought piles of recently printed posters and leaflets bearing the words 'Help Us Find Shannon' and a picture of her smiling that shy grin. Kids and adults alike began to rip up the posters and toss them in the air, delighted that they would now never be needed. Soon it appeared to be snowing paper as the sky filled with scraps of white poster bearing snatches of Shannon's face. The constant gusts of chill spring breeze tossed them up and down the street like tickertape until everyone was dancing ankle-deep in paper.

As the drinking intensified, one overexcited local did a streak down Moorside Avenue. And as with all alcohol-soaked affairs there was a potentially ugly element too. When a ball signed by the Bradford Bulls rugby club during Shannon's disappearance went missing, a man on the public address system warned the culprit to return it or have the 'shit kicked out of him'.

Later on, the party drifted up the road to the Community House where the last reveller finally crawled home at around 6.00am. It had been quite a night.

Far away from the noise and hullabaloo of the celebrations, little Shannon had settled down at a secret safe house for another night spent with strangers and hidden from the world. It had been an extraordinary day for her: waking up again at Lidgate Gardens, rushing to hide under Mike's double bed when the door crashed open, and then the astonishing moment she pushed herself free and was picked up and carried into the daylight by the burly detective. And then there was the police station, all the men and women in uniforms smiling at her and knowing her name without her even needing to tell them. And the medical checks to make sure she was OK and that Mike hadn't hurt her.

Although unharmed, Shannon appeared exhausted. At that stage, it was too early for the results of medical tests which would reveal that her sleepiness and lethargy were due to all the drugs she had been fed. Instead, the carers just thought she must be simply overwrought by recent events. They chatted and played with her and, thankfully, that night for Shannon was very different to those of the last few weeks. Even different to those of the last few years. That night she was secure, being cared for by people who sat and laughed with her as they watched a DVD together, tucked her snugly into bed and watched over her as she drifted off to sleep. Shannon was safe.

15

THE MORNING
AFTER

It seemed the whole of Dewsbury Moor had a thick head as day broke on Saturday, 15 March. Moorside Avenue was littered with empty lager cans and bottles of cheap fizzy wine. The shredded 'Help Us Find Shannon' leaflets were now blown all round the gardens and kerbsides. Down the road, a fraction of Shannon's smile, one of her eyes or the scrunchy in her hair would be visible on the wayward scraps of paper. It seemed Shannon was everywhere, although in reality Shannon was nowhere near Moorside and probably never would be again.

Slowly, residents emerged from their homes, feeling the effects of partying until the early hours. They came out clutching mugs of strong sweet tea, still in their pyjamas, laughing with neighbours about the previous night's events. The morning's newspapers were passed round and they pointed at pictures of themselves, drinking and laughing, taken the previous evening.

Away from the Moor, though, the pictures had sparked

outrage in some quarters. How could it be proper for people to mark a little girl's horrific ordeal by drinking themselves into a frenzy? There were comments about the way some of the locals looked – their lack of teeth, their obesity and their cheap, ill-fitting clothes. One sniffy piece of editorial commented that 'a feral element was out in force' during the celebrations. But the residents of Dewsbury Moor let it wash over them. They'd heard it all before – well-off 'snobs' having a go at them.

They were the ones who had lived with the uncertainty and stress for 24 days that one of their children was missing and might not come home. And now it was over they would celebrate in whatever way they wanted.

The clear-up operation at the Community House was soon under way with bottles, cans and old 'Find Shannon' posters bagged up awaiting the next bin collection. As they tidied, locals who had spent days and nights searching for the missing child reflected on what an extraordinary time it had been.

At 24 Moorside Avenue, there was no movement at all that morning. Karen and Craig still hadn't returned from their night in the hotel so there was little for the camera crews and press photographers to focus their lenses on. Local kids still in their Disney-character pyjamas offered reporters cups of tea to while away the hours. The spirit of togetherness in victory had still not left Dewsbury Moor.

Photographers were desperate to catch the moment Karen returned home, hopefully at which point she would pose for pictures and might even reveal something about her daughter's ordeal. The media and the public alike were desperate to know what had really been going on during Shannon's time in captivity. As were the police.

By midday on Saturday, it was felt the time was right to begin gently questioning the little girl.

Shannon Matthews had woken looking and feeling more refreshed. She had slept well despite the confusion of the past few days and the effects of some of the sleeping pills would have been beginning to wear off.

She was given a healthy, hearty breakfast and allowed to spend time playing with a little kitten she had been given to take her mind away from everything that had happened. Those caring for her felt she was already 'well on her way to recovery' after her ordeal, so, after a couple of hours spent playing and chatting with carers, she was taken into the specially designed police suite where young victims of crime were questioned. The room had been designed to look like a school classroom, and it was there that the conversations about what had happened began. Questioning took place in bursts of no more than 15 minutes, allowing Shannon regular breaks from reliving the confusion and horror of the past few weeks.

There was also a child psychologist on hand to help minimise any distress, because the detectives and psychologists were all too conscious of the potential damage of adding to Shannon's sense of trauma if the questioning was not handled correctly. In fact, it soon became apparent that Shannon was quite deeply damaged by what had happened, both before and during her period of captivity.

Over the next few days, she suffered recurring hallucinations about her time away from home. For some time, she was convinced she had been held captive by her real father, Leon Rose, the man she had begged to go and stay with before her disappearance. She had also thought that, when police burst into the flat to rescue her, it was actually Craig Meehan coming to save her.

The police quickly realised Shannon wasn't making up the stories – she truly believed them. She also told them about a trip to the seaside and to a market during the kidnap period. And she was unable to tell police how many brothers and sisters she had – becoming convinced her younger sister was older than her.

Officers didn't yet realise the amount of drugs she had been given which could have affected her thinking. But it soon became apparent that it was going to be extremely difficult to use Shannon's evidence in court because she was so deeply confused.

In a hotel far from Dewsbury Moor, Karen Matthews was waking up to the reality that her dream of bagging a £50,000 reward for her missing daughter was over. Beyond that, she must have known it would be only a matter of time until her full involvement in the plot was revealed. So, at a time when she must surely have felt at her lowest ebb for 24 days, the rest of the world was expecting to see her ecstatic and delirious that her daughter had been found safe and well.

The police family liaison officers again spent time with her that day. On the face of it, they were supposed to be keeping Karen up to date with Shannon's condition and developments in the investigation. In reality, they were keeping a close watch on her every move.

'Were you having an affair with Michael Donovan?' Det Con Christine Freeman asked Karen suddenly that day.

But there was not a hint of outrage or shock at the officer's question. 'He's not good-looking enough for me,' Karen laughed.

'And Craig is?' Det Con Freeman quipped back.

The pair both laughed conspiratorially. Det Con Freeman knew she had to retain a good-natured relationship with Karen if she were ever to get a confession from her about her part in Shannon's disappearance.

It was evening when Karen and Craig eventually returned to Moorside Avenue. As the police car carrying them pulled up outside their home and they walked hand-in-hand towards the front door accompanied by two CID officers, the click of camera shutters and cries from photographers for the couple to 'look this way', 'look at each other' and 'give her a kiss' almost drowned out the screaming and cheering from neighbours. But not quite. They were clapped and wolf-whistled by their friends and neighbours like returning heroes.

The couple went into their house then came out and posed for pictures on the slight slope of their front path. Karen was wearing a body-hugging striped jumper, which made her look thinner than usual. Her face was drawn and she appeared exhausted – none of the strain of the last weeks seemed to have left her face. In fact, she looked desperately worried and gripped Craig's hand tightly the entire time. Finally, Julie Bushby, who was already inside their house, had to yell out the front door to Karen, 'Look happy!'

It was only then that Karen broke into a broad grin and the camera shutters went crazy – finally getting the picture they wanted. Twice then, on the yelled requests of the photographers, they turned and kissed.

As they stood in the glare of the flashbulbs, reporters called out questions, desperate for any scrap of new information, but little was forthcoming. Asked how she felt on seeing Shannon again, Karen said she was 'overwhelmed'. 'I just couldn't stop crying,' she went on, 'knowing she's back where she belongs and she's safe. I never gave up hope and now she'll be able to come home and sleep in her room again. We've got her new pink bedding which she'll love. The police have helped a lot. We can't thank them enough.'

Asked about support from the local community, she said it had been 'fantastic'. 'We're just happy to be a family again,' she added. 'That's all we've wanted – Shannon back and safe – now the family is safe again.'

Although locals knew Karen hadn't yet been able to even touch her missing daughter and that she was being held under a protection order, everyone still believed it was simply police process. No one had yet considered that Shannon might not ever be coming home.

But, as the initial shock and jubilation that Shannon had been found began to subside, there followed a period of questioning and recrimination. On the estate and in the press, fingers were pointed at the police. Why had it taken them so long to find Shannon? Surely Michael Donovan was no criminal mastermind capable of foiling West Yorkshire's finest detective minds for weeks on end? And didn't everyone know that when kids went missing it was almost always a family member that was responsible?

At the same time, a number of people came forward saying they had alerted officers to Michael Donovan days and even weeks earlier. Ryan Baynes, a father-of-two, claimed he had called police shortly after Shannon's disappearance to tell them Michael had behaved strangely at a family funeral six weeks earlier, bouncing Shannon on his knee and paying her 'far too much attention'.

And one of Michael's neighbours, Melvin Glew, said that around midday on 8 March – a week before Shannon was found – he rang the Missing People charity's number, printed on hundreds of posters around Dewsbury. He told the operator that he had become suspicious of Michael, whose flat was 100 yards from his, because he had begun acting oddly ever since Shannon disappeared and, while formerly a man of strict routines, his daily rituals had changed. Lights that had previously always been left on were switched off, and those that had previously always been off were now on.

And the long hours Michael had previously spent washing and polishing his car had suddenly stopped. Mr Glew also knew about Michael's bitter custody battle for his children and it only fuelled his concerns. But his suspicions only came to a head when he spotted a man trying to visit his neighbour in a car with 'Find Shannon' posters in the windows. Michael hadn't answered the door, even though Mr Glew was convinced he was at home.

'I was dead suspicious,' recalled Mr Glew, a forklift driver. 'I rang the helpline number and said it would be a good idea if the police got into his house and had a look. I gave them his address but nobody got back to me and I heard nothing more. I was really surprised it took them this long to get round to searching his place. Thank God they did.'

The Missing People charity confirmed it had passed on the address, although it remained unclear what the timescale was between Mr Glew's initial call and the information being processed and sent to the police.

Edward McMillan-Scott, the Conservative MEP for Yorkshire and Humberside, made no bones about his criticisms of the West Yorkshire Police Force. 'In more than three out of four cases like this, a family member is involved,' he said. 'Police should have conducted a thorough search that would have included the suspect.'

Wounded and angry that their massive multimillion-pound inquiry was now coming under attack, West Yorkshire Police hit back. Chief Superintendent Barry South said, 'Let me put on notice that, had we known at any time the whereabouts of Shannon, we would have been there within seconds. These people are now coming out of the woodwork.'

Sources within West Yorkshire Police also let it be known that more than 300 names had been entered on a family tree for Karen and Craig – most of whom had been interviewed – but Michael Donovan's details were never given to them. The Meehan family member living just a mile away with a history of child abduction and petty crime had simply slipped everyone's minds.

Alice Meehan – Michael's sister – immediately fell under suspicion. A uniformed officer was posted outside her door that Saturday and arrangements were made to interview her. But, despite living geographically near, Michael Donovan probably wasn't a close relative of the Meehans, although he had suddenly started visiting more frequently following Brian's death.

Neil Hyett, whose wife Amanda was Michael's niece, said he couldn't think why he had never considered mentioning him to officers. 'I can't believe we didn't think of him, he's not that close to us but we were at one point thinking about fostering his children,' he said.

Few neighbours on the estate recognised Michael as a regular visitor to the Meehans either. A couple knew him by sight from the working men's club in Batley, but that was about it.

West Yorkshire Chief Constable Sir Norman Bettison leaped to the defence of officers who had worked day after day in freezing cold conditions searching for Shannon but who were now coming under attack for the investigation. He praised their 'phenomenal and unprecedented professionalism' in the hunt saying he was 'immensely satisfied and immensely proud of them'.

Sir Norman went on to dismiss reports that police had been given comprehensive tip-offs about the flat in Lidgate Gardens. He said, 'The people that might have said, and have been quoted in the press, as having given the police the whole jigsaw puzzle – the box lid – are fantasising.'

In fact, even with Shannon safe and Michael in custody, there were still several parts of the jigsaw missing.

By late in the day on Sunday, 6 March, almost 48 hours since Shannon's rescue, people were beginning to wonder why Karen Matthews hadn't been allowed to see her daughter again; surely they couldn't still be doing forensic tests on her clothes? And even if Shannon was undergoing questioning, why couldn't her mother be present too? Doubts began to surface in the minds of people on the estate – and across the country.

Karen and Craig hadn't left home since returning on the Saturday evening, but a statement was issued on Karen's behalf by West Yorkshire Police. Its contents revealed that the police – if not Karen – knew exactly what people must be thinking. Sounding nothing like the way Karen normally spoke, the statement said, 'I know that people in the community and the media are wondering when

Shannon will be able to come back home to be with us. I fully understand that the police need to keep speaking to Shannon to establish exactly what has happened during the time that she has been missing. I appreciate that could take some time and is not something that is going to happen overnight.

'The most important thing is that Shannon is safe. I have seen Shannon and I am completely happy that she is being very well looked after and is being given all the care she needs. Of course I want her back with us as soon as that's possible but I understand that could take some time. When she does come home I want it to be for good. Our main priority is Shannon's welfare.'

Later, talking to the *Yorkshire Evening News* in language which sounded a lot more convincing and natural, she added, 'I know the police have got to do what they have got to do. But I can't wait to have my daughter back. When we do get Shannon back home with us, we will plan a bit of a party to welcome her home and we will be involving all the community in that to thank them for all their support.'

But Leon Rose's response sounded far more like the spontaneous eruption of a parent whose worst fears had been proved wrong. He said he was still 'buzzing' over the news and couldn't wait to see Shannon. 'I'll grab hold of her and give her a cuddle and tell her I love her,' he said. 'I'm thankful that the nightmare is over – it's now a dream come true.'

The following morning, an air of normality returned to Dewsbury Moor for the first time in almost four weeks. It was a Monday morning and those with jobs set off for the first time in ages with a lighter heart. The kids were back at school. Even Karen and Craig appeared to be regaining a more normal rhythm to their life – getting their family liaison officers to drop them at Asda for some food shopping. Walking down the aisles, shoppers turned to stare at the pair who had become local celebrities.

The family liaison officers asked Karen if she'd like to buy her daughter a welcome-home present which they would pass on to her. The thought had never occurred to Karen herself but after a while browsing the radio-controlled cars she finally chose a new Bratz doll for Shannon. They left laden with food, bags of lager... and the solitary doll.

From there, Karen asked to be taken to a gaming shop. After that, they headed home with Karen still sitting silently in the back of the car, not asking officers any questions about how Shannon was feeling or when she would be reunited with her.

Meanwhile, Michael Donovan was undergoing another day of questioning at Halifax Police Station. The police applied for and received an extension to the amount of time they could hold him without a charge being brought. They were keen to amass as much evidence as they could before charging him.

All day long, officers consulted with the Crown Prosecution Service (CPS) about the strength of their case. With such a high-profile situation, they couldn't afford any mistakes – they had to be sure they had enough evidence for a conviction on the charges they laid down. The questioning of Shannon was also continuing as officers probed delicately into what had happened to her.

Typically, children are difficult witnesses because they

find it harder to judge times and distances and they can struggle to recall exact conversations. But in Shannon's case this was made all the more difficult because she had spent most of her time at Lidgate Gardens drugged into a state of sleepiness and confusion. But on one issue she was very clear. When Shannon was asked the most obvious question of all – did she want to see her mother? – the simple answer came back: 'No.'

That day, the Emergency Police Protection Order expired and Shannon was transferred without any contest to the care of Kirklees Social Services which became responsible for finding her a foster home.

As dusk turned to darkness, tensions were mounting in the back offices at Halifax Police Station. A charge had to be brought against Donovan soon – and it had to stand up in court.

Finally, just before 10.00pm, detectives stopped the questioning. With or without Donovan's cooperation in interview, they were confident they had enough evidence to charge him. Around 15 minutes later, Peter Mann, head of the CPS's Complex Case Unit, addressed a press conference at Dewsbury Police Station. He appeared nervous and hot in front of the camera lights and focused hard as he read from a lengthy statement. But it was only the last lines that really interested anyone: 'Having carefully considered all the material supplied to us by West Yorkshire Police, we have made the decision there is sufficient evidence and made the decision that Michael Donovan is charged with kidnapping and false imprisonment.'

Donovan was set to appear before Dewsbury Magistrates Court first thing the following morning. Then the world would see the social misfit behind the abduction of little Shannon.

16

CRAIG UNDER ARREST

As Michael Donovan stood in the clean, modern dock at Dewsbury Magistrates Court on Tuesday, 18 March, one question was surely spinning through the minds of everyone who looked at him: How could this man possibly be capable of carrying out such an audacious plan all on his own? Michael was certainly very far from the picture of a master criminal. He shuffled into the dock barely able to walk and as white as chalk. His bulbous eyes and gaunt cheeks made him appear a good 20 years older than his real age of 39. Dressed in a dark-blue sweatshirt and grey trousers, he appeared tiny next to the four security guards surrounding him.

The hearing was over in just five minutes and Michael spoke only to confirm his name, address and date of birth. In the public gallery, Amanda Hyett burst into tears at the start of the hearing. She was comforted by husband Neil and Julie Bushby who seemed to be representing all the people of Dewsbury Moor who had worked so hard to find Shannon.

Michael was remanded in custody to appear via videolink at Leeds Crown Court on 26 March, before being led back to the cells in handcuffs. As the security van accelerated away from the back of the courthouse to take him to Armley Jail in Leeds, a small but noisy group of protesters jeered and shouted, 'Scum,' as loudly as they could. But police were determined no protesters would get near the van and had created a cordon around the access road.

With Michael heading north towards Armley – an imposing Victorian building known for its tough regime – the angry residents of Dewsbury Moor were left catching the bus home, wondering whether this really was the end of the saga. With every hour that passed, it really did seem just too much to believe that social misfit and loner Michael Donovan could have managed to mastermind and get away with the plot single-handedly. And even if he had, why? What was his motive? There had been no charges related to sexual abuse of the girl and police sources were saying she had been unharmed. Nothing seemed to make sense.

To the 60 West Yorkshire Police detectives still working on the case, it was making far greater sense – they were now convinced Karen had planned the whole thing. And her motive was money. But they still needed to prove it.

Karen Matthews clearly knew fingers of suspicion were being pointed at her by the police, neighbours and journalists alike. So, on the day Michael appeared before magistrates, she launched her own last-ditch attempt to throw the doubters off her scent. In an exclusive front-page interview with the *Yorkshire Evening Post* headlined 'Shannon's mum: We were not involved', she hit back at rumours that had been appearing in other papers.

'I would like to say how hurtful and unhelpful the tone of some of the press coverage has been,' she was quoted as saying. 'At a time when me and my family are under a massive amount of stress, some of the stories have only added to the pain we are all feeling. Please bear this in mind when writing or reporting about a very difficult and personal time in our lives.'

Karen was still playing the role of wounded mother to the full. That evening, she was due to lead a tree-planting ceremony at the front of her house in honour of Shannon and to mark the fourth week since she had disappeared. But the police had other ideas. Detectives who had been questioning Shannon felt it was time to speak to Karen and Craig officially, and they were brought in by their family liaison officers. The tree-planting ceremony was postponed until the following day.

As Karen set off back to Dewsbury Police Station, her friends went to great lengths to say she was going voluntarily and had not been arrested. She was simply helping out with routine enquiries, the friends insisted. But face-to-face with detectives probing the circumstances of Shannon's disappearance, Karen can have been left in little doubt that there were now grave suspicions about the part she may have played in it. There were certainly plenty of questions detectives now wanted answered.

Although not under arrest, Karen was interviewed under caution – meaning it was a formal tape-recorded interview but she was free to leave at any time. The interview took place in a relaxed, living-room setting, complete with armchair, coffee table and even a floral wallpaper border on the wall.

But, despite the homely atmosphere, detectives went

about their questioning with steely determination. Throughout the meeting, Karen sat slouched in her green parka jacket, growing increasingly flushed in the face as she deflected the accusations thrown at her.

She began by giving officers her own version of events, explaining why she believed Michael would have snatched her daughter. She told how she and Craig had rowed at Brian Meehan's funeral and so she had gone to his mum Alice's house. It was there that she got talking to Michael and started telling him about her problems. 'He offered me a place to stay with the kids until Craig calmed down,' Karen told officers. 'I said, "No, I don't want to go, I need to talk things through with Craig." That's the reason he's done this,' she said firmly. 'I could have protected her from him.'

Karen was then asked directly if she had known where Shannon was all along – but there was no way she was giving up her act yet. 'I swear on my life I did not,' she told the officers. 'If I knew where she was I would have gone and grabbed her myself. I wouldn't have wasted police time if I'd known where she was. I'm a weak person, I'm not a strong person. I never thought he [Michael] was like that. What he's done had shocked us all.'

Even when asked why she had failed to mention Michael's existence to officers trying to build up family trees, Karen had an answer: 'I thought you were on about close friends and family which Mick wasn't really. He wasn't that close.' Then Karen claimed she hadn't even realised Craig was related to Michael, thinking he was just a family friend.

Karen also confided that Craig had feared she would dump him because he was related to Michael but that she'd told him, 'I'm not going to take it out on you.'

It was a convincing performance. Her vigorous self-defence made some officers think that maybe she was innocent after all and Michael was simply trying to squirm his way out of the situation by pointing the finger at her. But others were frustrated by Karen's self-pitying nature and the way she ladled out blame towards everyone else. At one point she even attempted to point the finger at her own parents, June and Gordon.

Det Con Andy Simpson was quizzing her on why, during the hunt, she'd said she believed someone close to her might be responsible. 'My mum has tried to abduct Shannon before. I thought my parents had something to do with it,' she said. So why hadn't she told police this at the time? Again, Karen retreated into her shell of self-pity: 'Because at the end of the day it doesn't matter what I say.'

Karen may have returned home thinking she had done a good job of convincing detectives of her innocence but she must have been shocked and shaken by the depth and breadth of their questioning. And she was certainly no closer to seeing Shannon.

When the tree-planting ceremony got under way the following evening, Karen appeared awkward and uncomfortable, as if desperate to bolt back at the earliest opportunity behind the front door of No 24, which she had left wide open. Children from Westmoor Junior lined up quietly with neighbours as local vicar Kathy Robertson led a short informal service thanking God for the safe return of Shannon. Speaking softly in the chill spring air, she also praised the hard work of local people in refusing to ever give up on Shannon during her abduction.

Then the young magnolia tree was gently lowered into the ground by Shannon's brothers to a round of applause from the watching crowd. Julie Bushby had come up with the idea as a way of marking Shannon's safe return and to thank everyone who had tried so hard to find her. 'It is to welcome Shannon back when she comes home,' Julie said.

How shocked residents would have been then to know Shannon would never return to that street.

Finally, Karen, dressed in a turquoise sports top and looking pale and shaken, read a few words from a scrap of paper ripped from a school exercise book: 'Thank you to everyone in the community for everything they have done. We are grateful to all the people from around the country for the time and effort they put in to find Shannon. She is safe and well and that is all that matters.'

Craig stood at her shoulder emotionless, wearing a white football hoodie and his ubiquitous Rockport cap pulled down firmly. Then they were gone, back into their front room, now being guarded by a Police Community Support Officer, and away from the cameras and the increasingly suspicious glances of their neighbours.

But any privacy Karen might have hoped for in her own home was blown away the following day when Channel 4 screened a fly-on-the-wall *Cutting Edge* documentary which had been filmed with Karen and Craig while Shannon was still missing. At the time, Karen had perhaps hoped the documentary would endear her to the public.

Throughout the hour-long film there were repeated mentions of the family's poverty and the little attention Shannon's story had received compared to that of Madeleine McCann. But, with the programme being aired now that Shannon had been found, Karen must have feared that it only served to give viewers an insight into her life which in many unguarded moments did her few favours. In one scene, she was shown moaning about photographers that she had invited in to raise the profile of the 'Missing Shannon' campaign. In another, she and Craig explained why they weren't out actively helping in the search because: 'They [the police] don't want us to go out there in case if there were anything there we would destroy it basically.'

After pausing to shovel more takeaway from a Styrofoam box into her mouth, Karen continued, 'They will have more detail of what to look for than what we have.' It sounded barely plausible.

But, as the next few days passed by, articles in the papers about Karen and Shannon Matthews gradually ebbed away. There were other stories, other tragedies, other mysteries, and finally a strange kind of peace returned to Dewsbury Moor. Karen's other children returned to school and Craig gradually went back to work on the fish counter at Morrisons. Julie Bushby got on with dealing with residents' everyday worries and concerns.

Some locals did think it strange, though, that Karen still hadn't seen Shannon since the day she was found and there was a strong smell of suspicion in the air. At Dewsbury Police Station, the major investigation team was still working gruelling hours trying to piece together the final pieces of the jigsaw.

Family liaison officers also stayed in regular contact with Karen, gradually attempting to tease out information. During one casual chat with Karen, family liaison officer Det Con Alex Grummitt asked whether Craig had ever hit her. 'No,' she replied. But when asked if she'd ever hit him, Karen admitted, 'Yes, loads of times.'

Checks had also been made into Craig's computer, which had been seized the day after Shannon's disappearance, to see whether she had been communicating with any potential abductor over the internet. There was no sign of Shannon having an unsuitable friendship – but officers did find some other horrific images.

Computer experts were soon able to tell that someone had been regularly using the computer to access child pornography. There were 653 recorded references on the hard drive to 'Lolita' – a name regularly used by perverts to access sexual images of the young. Some of the images viewed had involved children as young as four. And some were so indecent they were categorised towards the highest end of the scale in which such offences are measured.

The decision was taken that there was enough evidence to arrest Meehan immediately. Early on the morning of 3 April, plain-clothes detectives banged on the door of 24 Moorside Road. Karen and Craig were used to police visits by this time – but neither can have been prepared for this. Craig was being arrested on suspicion of possessing indecent images of children.

He was driven away to Dewsbury Police Station, leaving Karen shocked and stunned. It was the last time she is believed to have seen him. Surely she must have feared the knock on the door that morning had been for her. But, no, it was Craig who was this time taken off for questioning. Within hours, news of Craig's arrest had spread around the Moor like an out-of-control bushfire.

Friends and neighbours, who had unreservedly backed Karen and Craig throughout Shannon's disappearance and all the rumours, were gutted. Questions raced through everyone's minds. Could the pictures involve any of Karen's children? And if so, could that mean Craig had been involved in a plot to abduct Shannon. The thinking was very much, 'If he was capable of watching child pornography, what else might he have done?'

Petra Jamieson recalled feeling 'sick, sick to my stomach'.

Many people on Dewsbury Moor were well acquainted with crime; statistics showed it had well above the national average. But that was good 'honest' crime: burglary, benefits fiddling and shoplifting. What Craig was accused of – looking at sex pictures of kids – was beyond the pale. Everyone was appalled.

Some people made threats that Craig could face vigilantes if he attempted to return home. One resident said, 'He wouldn't last a minute. People on this estate act first and ask questions later. He may be innocent, but these folk won't wait for a judge and jury. They feel betrayed and are very angry.'

But in a few quarters there were those still prepared to give Craig the benefit of the doubt. In Moorside Road, where people were constantly in and out of each other's houses, Craig's computer was regularly used by dozens of people. Petra told how she had even used it herself. 'The police need to check times and dates for the different people that have used the computer,' said Petra.

That, of course, was what they were doing as they questioned Craig at Dewsbury Police Station about his work schedules and the dates and times that he had been at home. While Craig underwent questioning, Karen was nowhere to be seen that day. Few people knew the real reason – she was having her first proper meeting with Shannon since her disappearance.

It was 20 days since Karen had even seen her daughter but finally Shannon had agreed to a meeting. Karen showed barely a flicker of excitement as family liaison officer Det Con Christine Freeman drove her to the rendezvous point. Instead, Karen demanded that they stop at the Post Office so she could collect her benefits. Then she moaned she was hungry and the pair had to drive round looking for a sandwich shop.

Det Con Freeman was appalled. 'All this while her "princess" was waiting for her,' she recalled. But things were only to get worse. 'When I led her to the room where Shannon was, she seemed numb. We were in there for three hours, most of it in silence. "Tell her you've missed her," I screamed in my head.'

But Karen couldn't – or wouldn't. As the minutes dragged by, Karen watched as Shannon played in a sandpit and did some painting. But there was little communication between the two and even less sign of a deep mother/daughter bond. Afterwards, Karen stunned Det Con Freeman by saying, 'That went well.' Karen appeared to have no idea how to be a loving mother – even when she was acting.

Karen was then taken to a safe house. With the new allegations against Craig, tensions were running high in Dewsbury Moor and it was felt it was best for her to stay away. By the following morning, Craig had been charged and presented at Dewsbury Magistrates Court on 11 charges of possessing 130 indecent images of youngsters. Fourteen of the pictures were said to show adults having sex with children as young as 11. Others showed children aged just four performing sex acts. None of the pictures involved any family members.

Again there was a smattering of locals from the Moorside estate in the public gallery to witness events as Craig, wearing a black Manchester United away shirt emblazoned with the name Ronaldo on the back, stepped into the dock, looking even more docile and gormless than usual. He spoke only to give his name, address and age and to confirm he understood the charges against him. For the rest of the ten-minute hearing, he sat in sullen silence as the lawyers talked around him.

Prosecutor David Holderness told the court Craig faced 11 charges – one overall charge of possessing indecent images and ten specimen charges. Mr Holderness outlined to the court how Craig's computer had been seized in the hope it might provide a clue to Shannon's whereabouts during her disappearance. But, although it hadn't done that, it had provided evidence of other offences being carried out.

Craig was clearly all too aware of the attitude of the Moor's residents towards the sort of offences he was charged with. As a result, his own solicitor, Robert Dawson, said he would not be applying for bail, believing Craig would be better off in custody. Mr Dawson said, 'Mr Meehan should remain in custody for his own protection and safety. In normal circumstances, I would be making a bail application and it wouldn't be opposed. The difference here is because of the publicity surrounding this case. The address that he has is not suitable to be put forward for the court. I cannot put forward a suitable address so he cannot make a bail application.' The case was adjourned until Friday, 11 April.

As Craig left court an hour and a half later, on the way to join his uncle in Armley Jail in Leeds, attention swung back to Karen. Had she known what her partner was doing on the computer? If not, how could she remain with him when she was herself the mother of young children?

Petra Jamieson and Julie Bushby were among the first at Karen's side, trying to support her through what they believed must be a terrible shock coming so soon after Shannon's abduction. As they hugged and tried to console her, Karen told them firmly, 'It's over. There's no way we can be together.'

Just weeks earlier, Karen had called Craig her 'rock' and defended him against slurs and rumours – now she was demanding her friends bag up his possessions and remove every trace of him from her life.

Whatever Karen might really have wanted herself, she must have realised the tide of popular feeling now raging against Craig. She had no choice but to dump him if she was to retain the public sympathy she so desperately still needed over Shannon's abduction. The last thing she wanted right then was more people asking difficult questions about her suitability as a mum.

'Karen has dumped Craig,' Petra told reporters after a meeting with her best pal at the safe house where she was staying. 'She doesn't want to be part of his life any more. She hasn't told him face-to-face, but I think he'll assume that anyway after what's gone on in the past 48 hours.

'She's obviously upset, but she's trying to keep her head up. I can't begin to imagine what's going on in her head. She must be feeling sick and disgusted. We're all sticking by her and want people to know that they should not take their anger out on her. She is entirely innocent and has done nothing wrong. She should not be blamed for anything.'

Julie Bushby added, 'She woke up on Wednesday morning excited about seeing Shannon but then her whole world collapsed. She is horrified about what's happened and cannot get over it. It's over between them. She's so confused, her life is in turmoil.'

Both Petra and Julie had been at Karen's side throughout the horrors of the last six weeks. They had seen her apparent suffering and her tears – and the way she acted in front and away from the cameras. And, although Julie still felt a deep well of sympathy for Karen, even she was becoming uncertain about some of her behaviour.

Then, just when it seemed the Moor couldn't possibly withstand another shock, there were more arrests the very next day – Friday, 4 April. CID officers called Craig's sister Amanda Hyett and mother Alice Meehan and made appointments for that morning for them to come along to Dewsbury Police Station.

Amanda's husband was away on a coach-driving job in Spain and she was alone when she entered the police station. But if she and her mother thought they were being asked along to discuss the charges being laid against Craig they were very wrong. Now the police were interested in them – and in connection with Shannon's abduction.

Amanda, 25, was arrested on suspicion of assisting an offender, while Alice Meehan, 49, was arrested on suspicion of attempting to pervert the course of justice. The new arrests were the worst blow to Dewsbury Moor yet. That people who had been at the very centre of the hunt for Shannon were being questioned by police seemed unthinkable. Neighbours began viewing each other with suspicion, the inevitable questions circling their minds – just how well did they know any of their neighbours after all? And, what exactly were any of them capable of doing?

Petra Jamieson told how, ever since Craig's arrest early

on Wednesday morning, it almost seemed like the ground was moving beneath the feet of the Moor's residents. There was no certainty about anything any more. 'Before Wednesday we seemed to get back to a bit of normality,' she said. 'There was no press and then on Wednesday morning I got a phone call and came outside and thought, "What's happened?" It's been more confusing than anything else, it's still not sinking in for many of us. One minute we're on a high, the next minute we're brought right back down.'

Amanda and Alice were questioned by detectives under caution for several hours before being released on police bail. They were then driven home by officers as neighbours strained to catch a glimpse of this very latest drama on the estate. The women were later questioned again before being released without charge. But, although they were eventually deemed entirely innocent of all the charges, huge damage was done to their reputations that week.

There was a definite mood of 'no smoke without fire' sweeping the streets of Dewsbury Moor. But that weekend far, far more shocking news was to come.

17
EVERYONE WILL HATE ME

At her safe house, Karen Matthews must have been feeling increasingly isolated. Michael Donovan and Craig Meehan were both behind bars, her family had disowned her, and her friends back on Dewsbury Moor were increasingly bewildered by her behaviour.

It seemed like the police were picking off their targets one by one. She must surely have wondered how long it would be until the knock came at her door. But still, even in front of her closest friends, she had to keep up the charade she had been acting out for almost two months. The strain was beginning to tell.

Friends Julie Bushby and Natalie Brown – who had put Karen up when her home was being forensically examined immediately after Shannon's disappearance – had become particularly concerned about inconsistencies in Karen's story and the strange swings in her behaviour. Natalie felt Karen was now constantly changing her story and contradicting herself.

Natalie and Julie talked things over time and again – comparing and contrasting the stories Karen had told them at different times. They discussed too how Karen always seemed more distraught when the TV cameras were around, and how her relationship with Craig just didn't seem quite right.

On Sunday, 6 April, Det Con Christine Freeman received a phone call from Julie Bushby. The caller broke the news with her usual no-nonsense brusqueness. 'Natalie and I think Karen's story is dodgy,' Julie told Det Con Freeman.

Christine quickly thought through the best course of action, then agreed with Julie that she would collect Karen from her safe house and drive her to meet the two women where they could confront her directly with their concerns. The rendezvous point was fixed for 6.00pm in a car park in Batley town centre.

When Christine and Karen arrived in the car park, Julie and Natalie were already waiting. They climbed into the backseat, looking enquiringly at Karen who was already in the front passenger seat, staring thoughtfully out of the window.

The women were inside just a couple of minutes when Natalie blurted out, 'Karen, I don't believe you, you're hiding something from me. I reckon you wanted to leave Craig so you told Michael to take care of Shannon, but you bottled it so you reported her missing.'

There was a silence lasting barely seconds. But for the women in that car it felt like hours. Then Karen took a deep breath. 'The biggest intake of breath that I've ever heard in my life,' Det Con Freeman recalled.

Finally, Karen spoke. 'Yes, that's right,' she whispered and slowly tears, real genuine tears, began to brim up in her eyes then spill down her face. She was shaking violently and for the first time looked truly terrified. But even then it was unclear whether the tears were for the damage she had done to Shannon or for herself.

Karen began panicking and babbling, trying desperately to explain to her two friends sitting stunned on the back seat what had happened. She told how she had been planning to leave Craig and take the children with her and had packed her bags ready to go but then Shannon hadn't turned up at the end of the road and she couldn't go through with it so she went home where Craig was waiting and had to report Shannon missing to cover her back.

She claimed she'd never had an affair with Michael – and didn't even have his phone number – but said he'd offered her a place to stay if she was considering leaving Craig. Babbling on and on, Karen's story changed within minutes. Next she said she had arranged for Michael to have Shannon for a couple of days to 'keep her safe while she and Craig could sort out her problems'. Through loud sobs, she pleaded with her friends to believe she had never meant for it to be an abduction.

To her friends who had seen Karen cry countless times over the past couple of months, there was a clear difference in these tears. 'It was the first time I had actually heard her cry that way. It was real tears, not crocodile tears,' Julie Bushby recalled.

'I didn't abduct my own daughter,' she wailed.

Next, Karen claimed she'd thought Michael would return Shannon after a day or so but he didn't and things then spiralled out of control, with her apparently unable to fathom a way of bringing it all to an end.

Her heart pounding, Christine Freeman stepped out of

the car, pulled out her mobile phone and called her boss to tell him of the events of the last few extraordinary minutes. A few seconds later, she sat back down in the driver's seat and turned to face Karen.

'Karen Matthews, you are under arrest for abduction,' Det Con Freeman said slowly.

But within seconds Karen was on the defensive and changed her story again. 'It wasn't me, it was Craig,' she kept saying. 'He arranged it with Michael.' She also blamed Craig's mother Alice for making the arrangement for Michael to look after Shannon.

'I wasn't involved in the abduction,' Karen insisted through her loud sobs. 'I just thought he was going to keep her overnight. I didn't think he'd keep her that long.'

Finally Karen's thoughts returned, as ever, to herself. 'People will hate me for what I've done and I've disgraced the kids,' she cried. 'What's going to happen to me now? I can't stand being in a cell.'

Christine drove Karen straight to Dewsbury Police Station, calling ahead for the custody unit to be cleared for privacy. After spending endless hours with Karen Matthews since the first day of Shannon's abduction, she couldn't help but feel some sympathy for the woman falling apart by her side. The custody officer said there was no way the suite could be cleared but Christine managed to find a private spot where Karen could sit away from the prying eyes of members of the public. 'I worked with her for a long time. I didn't want to see her upset,' Det Con Freeman later told Leeds Crown Court during Karen's trial.

At the police station, Karen continued to come up with a variety of excuses in her bid to explain away what had happened. At one point, totally unprompted, she told Det

Con Freeman, 'As far as I'm concerned, he's abducted her off his own back – people are putting words in my mouth.'

Just 20 minutes later, she said, 'I wasn't involved in the abduction. I just thought he was going to keep her overnight. I didn't think he was going to keep her that long. I'm never going to get my babies back together now.'

The news began to leak out late that Sunday night that Karen had been arrested. The police statement that a 32-year-old woman from Dewsbury Moor had been arrested on suspicion of perverting the course of justice left few in doubt as to who the police had picked up now. It must have been a cold, long night for Karen Matthews as she settled down in a cell that evening. However great her self-delusion, even she must have realised that public sympathy with her was now over – and no matter how many excuses she came up with, the damage had been done.

Twelve miles away at Armley Jail, Michael Donovan was clearly suffering similar anguish – because just hours after Karen's arrest he attempted to kill himself. Detectives don't believe he knew about Karen's arrest at the time, it was just a terrible coincidence. According to prison authorities, it was 'a serious attempt at self-harm'. Michael was found in a pool of his own blood in his cell having slit his wrists. He was taken to Leeds General Infirmary where he remained overnight.

On the morning of Monday, 7 April, Karen was transferred to Wakefield Police Station where she underwent lengthy interviews. Magistrates extended the time detectives were allowed to hold her, enabling them to comb through events of the last six weeks again and again and again, tackling Karen on the inconsistencies in her story. But the more they questioned her, the more complicated her story became in many ways – as she repeatedly contradicted herself, cast blame in every direction but her own and concocted more and more elaborate stories.

Karen initially insisted she had only asked Donovan to look after Shannon for a day. She said she'd asked him for help in leaving Craig the day before Shannon's disappearance when he had driven to Moorside Road to talk through the situation with her. 'I just wanted to know how to get him [Craig] out of my life because I didn't love him any more. I asked Mike for advice,' said Karen, slumped in her chair in the police interview room.

She said she asked him to take Shannon first because she was only nine and she did not want her to be hurt by her relationship breaking up. Karen then said she had planned to follow on with her other children. 'I asked him to pick Shannon up and I'd meet him somewhere with the rest of me and the kids with us stuff,' she said. 'When I'd got myself sorted out, I'd get in touch with him. But I could not go through with it in the end.'

She claimed she'd had no interest in reward money for her daughter, but she admitted Shannon knew nothing about the scheme. 'As far as she knew she was coming home to us,' Karen said. 'I just thought he was going to sit in his house and wait.'

When the interviewing officers asked why Karen had gone through with the call to the police, she claimed she had to: 'It was just to cover my own back really because Craig would have found out.' And when asked why she had never mentioned Michael's existence to officers trying to create a family tree, she responded, 'Because I didn't know him right much.'

Then came the million-dollar question: If the whole episode had just been an attempt to leave Craig which had become terribly out of control, why on earth hadn't she just confided in one of the family liaison officers with whom she had built close relationships. 'I wish I did now,' said Karen. 'I wanted to be strong for the children,' she went on, making no sense at all.

As the interviews continued, other detectives asked to see a copy of the TV programme *Shameless* which had been suggested as a blueprint for Karen's kidnap plan. They wanted to see if there really were similarities between the two plots. A video identity parade was also taking place in which a neighbour of Michael's identified Karen as a mystery woman she had spoken to outside his flat on 21 February – two days after Shannon went missing.

Carol Battye said she was walking down the path when a woman came out of Michael's doorway. 'She asked me if I knew what time Mick would be in,' Mrs Battye recalled, saying she then asked for a cigarette. She described the woman as between 30 and 40 years old, about 5ft 2ins with mousy hair. It was only after Shannon was found that she reflected back on the mystery woman and thought it could have been Karen she had seen that day.

Officers continued to question Karen at Wakefield Police Station throughout Monday and Tuesday. Some were growing frustrated by her constantly changing stories and the way she was casting blame around Dewsbury Moor like confetti. Then, on Tuesday, 8 April, Karen was charged with perverting the course of justice and child neglect. Even then, as the charge was read to her, Karen maintained her innocence. 'I didn't know where she was, I just knew who she was with,' she told officers.

The news was again released by Peter Mann, spokesman for the Crown Prosecution Service, who said, 'We have carefully considered all of the evidence in the file and decided there is sufficient evidence to charge Karen Matthews with perverting the course of justice and child neglect. We will continue to keep this case under constant review.' Mr Mann said, despite huge interest in the events surrounding Shannon Matthews, Ms Matthews 'has the right to a fair trial'. But, in a case which had received a huge amount of interest, that was to be easier said than done.

On Wednesday, 9 April, Karen made her first appearance before magistrates in Dewsbury in connection with the case. It was almost like history was repeating itself. Just five days earlier, Craig had stood in the same dock in the same court. And 17 days before that it had been the turn of Craig's uncle, Michael Donovan.

Outside the courtroom, in the neatly vacuumed, carpeted corridor, dozens of uniformed officers stood guard in case any unruly element should wish to take justice into their own hands. As a security van delivered her to the court, there were shouts and jeers and Karen can have been left in no doubt about people's feelings towards her.

Certainly, by the time she appeared in the dock handcuffed to two women officers, any last vestiges of colour had drained from her already pale face. She was left a mottled, white colour, making her red-rimmed eyes appear even more prominent. Wearing blue trousers and a dark-blue sweatshirt, Karen spent almost the entire hearing with her head bowed so her bushy auburn hair fell covering her face like a veil.

The courtroom was packed: reporters squeezed on to the press benches, senior officers in the case and Karen's family liaison officers sat at the sides, and Dewsbury Moor locals – including Julie Bushby, Natalie Brown, Neil and Amanda Hyett, Caroline Meehan and Petra Jamieson – bunched up close in the public gallery. Hardly an eye left Karen's stooped figure for the entire hearing, but with her thick hair hiding her features it was hard to gauge any reaction as two charges were read out of wilful neglect of a child and perverting the course of justice. Karen spoke only to confirm her name, address and give her date of birth.

The charges left no one in doubt as to the degree to which it was now thought Karen had been involved. The first charge was: 'On a day between the 18th day of February 2008 and the 15th day of March 2008 at Dewsbury being a person who had attained the age of 16 years and having responsibility for Shannon Matthews, a child under that age, namely nine years, wilfully neglected or abandoned the said child in a manner likely to cause unnecessary suffering to the said child or injury to her health.'

The second charge was: 'That you between the 18th day of February 2008 and the 15th day of March 2008 at Dewsbury, contrary to Common Law with intent to pervert the course of public justice, did a series of acts which had a tendency to pervert the course of public justice in that you repeatedly concealed information in relation to the whereabouts of Shannon Matthews in interviews and other contacts with officers with the West Yorkshire Police and claimed to have no knowledge of her whereabouts.'

Karen's solicitor Roger Clapham then took his chance and applied for bail on behalf of his client. He offered the address of a relative of Karen outside the immediate area, saying she was desperate to remain in contact with her children. But District Judge Jonathan Bennett refused the application and remanded Karen in custody – for her own safety and welfare. She was remanded in custody until 16 April, when she would appear by videolink at Leeds Crown Court at the same hearing as Michael Donovan.

Some Dewsbury Moor residents who had gathered in the court shouted 'Yes!' as Karen was remanded. She turned fleetingly towards them and shook her head as she was led away. The 13-minute hearing was over. As Karen was handcuffed and escorted from the court, she began talking to a security officer, again claiming Shannon's disappearance had been planned by Craig and other members of his family. But it was too late for Karen's excuses.

She was bundled into the back of another security van and driven slowly through the shouting crowd outside towards what would be her home for the near future – New Hall Prison near Wakefield. The Dewsbury Moor arrests weren't quite over yet though.

The next development was the re-arrest of Craig's sister Amanda Hyett and his mother Alice Meehan. The previous week it had been on suspicion of *attempting* to pervert the course of justice. This time, the pair and Craig's other sister, Caroline Meehan, were arrested on suspicion of perverting the course of justice. The trio were questioned by detectives at Dewsbury Police Station before being released on police bail pending further enquiries. But cases against the women were dropped and they were never charged with anything relating to Shannon's disappearance.

For people on the estate, it had reached a point where it

seemed the allegations and arrests might never stop. Although the claims of benefit fraud may not have bothered them unduly, they were horrified that six people had now been arrested in connection with Shannon's disappearance.

At Dewsbury Moor, feelings of anger towards Karen Matthews were matched by those of disbelief and confusion. How could she have put up such a convincing act for so long if she had known where her daughter was all along? And how could anyone have inflicted such a terrifying and disturbing experience on their own child?

Many people on the Moor had heard Karen's version of events blurted out in those first few moments after she was confronted by Natalie Brown in the back of Det Con Freeman's car. And that was the version many preferred to believe – that it had never been a premeditated abduction attempt, more just a stupid, stupid idea which had spun terribly out of control. It was felt that most likely Karen had been about to leave Craig to stay with Donovan – even if they weren't already having an affair. But then for some reason Karen lost her nerve at the last minute but wasn't able to tell Donovan in time and he had duly collected Shannon from the school bus as arranged. When she didn't return home and Craig asked where she was, Karen was then steam-rollered into reporting her missing.

But how Karen had managed to abandon her daughter for so long with a virtual stranger while millions of pounds were spent on searching for her confounded even her most sympathetic supporter.

Most of Karen's friends had now turned against her, angry that they too had been duped by her act and given up valuable time and effort searching for a little girl who was never really missing. But some did stand by Karen, and, although confused as to why she should have done such a thing, they felt she now needed their support more than ever and pledged to write to her in jail. However, one of the women being supportive was abused in the street and others became too fearful to discuss their sympathy for her publicly. The atmosphere at the Moor was turning ugly in parts and it was becoming a subject of concern for the police.

Within hours of Karen being remanded in custody, Kirklees Council contractors were boarding up No 24. The council had to keep Karen and Craig's house available for them because until their trials were concluded they remained innocent in the eyes of the law (if not those of their former neighbours). But concerns were mounting that the deserted house could become a target for vigilantes keen to express their sense of anger and betrayal with flying bricks or even petrol-filled bottles. So huge grey shutters were fixed over the windows as if drawing a metal veil over everything that had gone on inside there over the past six weeks.

In fact, the concern about violence breaking out on the estate led the police to station an officer outside the house even though it was now empty. In addition, uniformed officers walked all the local streets leafleting residents, urging them to resist taking matters into their own hands.

The leaflet tried hard to empathise with the bewilderment and anger residents were feeling, saying, 'We realise that people may be confused about recent events. We cannot go into detail about our investigation, but we would like to reassure you that we will find out the truth. It is important that the community does not jump to any conclusions about people who may be involved in this inquiry. Please do not take the law into your own hands and leave police to do their job.' It also thanked residents for their 'help and support' in the weeks since Shannon was reported missing.

The leaflets were the idea of Chief Inspector Vince Firth who also arranged for a meeting between residents and senior officers at Shannon's former school. More than 60 locals from the estate turned up in the desperate hope that someone might be able to help them make sense of the situation. Chief Insp Firth's message was chiefly one of trying to calm the community amid concerns that violence might break out against someone who may in fact be entirely innocent in the case.

He told the assembled meeting, 'One problem is that we have a few people who have been arrested but that does not mean they are guilty of anything. We have to investigate things and it's about saying to people don't jump to conclusions. We have got a lot of uncertainty.'

Chief Supt Barry South then went on to congratulate locals for all their hard work during the time when Shannon was missing. 'We are proud of you and nothing's going to change that,' he said. But he went on to emphasise how, having come through that experience, it was now imperative that the community stuck together. 'Whatever the outcome, whatever the anger, whatever your feelings are, for goodness sake, put them to one side. If I said to you on day one we will find Shannon but this is [what is] going to happen, you wouldn't have had that. For those of you who are thinking, "Right, we are not happy with this," it's done; that little girl is back with us.'

The officer's message seemed to hit a nerve and tensions on Dewsbury Moor subsided. And, as the days passed by with no further arrests or dramas, life for many residents did return to something closer to normality. The film crews and reporters departed because, with the story's key players – Karen and Craig – both in jail, there were few other people to focus upon.

People were just left waiting for the court cases to begin. At which point it was hoped everything would become clear. On 16 April, Karen Matthews appeared at Leeds Crown Court via videolink from New Hall Prison. She was seen sitting on a chair behind a table wearing a sky-blue T-shirt under a grey zipped top, with her red hair hanging loose over her shoulders. She looked deathly pale as she stared into the camera, speaking only to confirm her name and that she could hear the proceedings. It was Karen's first joint appearance with Michael, although he too didn't appear in person and was represented by his solicitor Malcolm Nowell.

Judge Peter Collier QC, Recorder of Leeds, adjourned the hearing for a plea and case management hearing in July and said the pair would face trial on 11 November. The following day, Karen, Craig and Donovan were all interviewed again by detectives in jail. This time, Karen simply handed over a prepared statement in which once again she laid the blame for everything that had happened at the door of Craig and his family.

It was to be a long, lonely seven months for Karen Matthews as she awaited trial and it soon became apparent she was not coping with prison life at all well. Inside jail, she was an easy target for other inmates. Her case had been all over the television and papers for months and Karen had become Britain's most notorious mother. To the other lags, such a crime against her own child was particularly abhorrent.

After just one night, Karen was moved to the segregation block where it was felt she could be monitored more effectively for her own safety. But that didn't stop the threats. 'We're going to get you! It's only a matter of time,' threatened one group of inmates. Other stories emerged that she had been threatened that her meals would be poisoned with bleach, glass or rat killer. And there was talk that a bounty of ten cigarettes had been placed on her head for anyone who 'got her'. Even to Karen, that must have seemed a pitifully small amount.

Friends who were keeping in contact with Karen said she was in fear for her life. She told them, 'I can't stand being in jail.' Her fear in prison led to a rapid decline in her mental health. Sources at the jail described her as 'extremely fragile' and 'badly affected' by the threats she was receiving. At the same time, Karen also had to come to terms with her children being taken into care – and the prospect that she might never see Shannon or any of them again. Social Services began securing care orders for Shannon's brothers and younger sister soon after Craig's first court appearance for possessing child pornography. Shannon had already been placed with foster parents and now similar loving homes were being identified for her siblings too. Scania the dog was living happily with Peter and Natalie Brown.

Karen became increasingly depressed and withdrawn and, within weeks, prison authorities were so concerned about her state that she was put on a 15-minute suicide watch. That meant she was checked by warders every quarter of an hour to make sure she hadn't harmed herself in any way. Karen found herself living alongside a child killer and a transsexual on New Hall's isolation wing – but she preferred it to having to watch her back every moment of every day alongside the other inmates, all of whom detested her.

The days passed with Karen watching television and scrawling letters to Shannon on A4 sheets of paper. The pages were littered with spelling mistakes and crossings-out as the barely literate mother attempted to send a message to her daughter which might possibly explain what she had done. It is not known whether any of the letters ever reached Shannon.

Michael was faring little better at Armley Prison. He too lived in constant fear of attacks from violent inmates keen to make a name for themselves by beating up such an infamous occupant of the jail. He spent a spell on a health wing where he was separated from other inmates.

Also at Armley, but separated from Michael, was his nephew Craig Meehan, still awaiting trail for possession of child pornography. Craig denied all the allegations against him and had chosen to be tried at Dewsbury Magistrates instead of the case being referred up to Crown Court. Despite concerns for his safety, he was so desperate to be free that he made repeated applications for bail – including one to an address just around the corner from Moorside Road where he claimed to have been offered a room. Perhaps Craig had no idea about the strength of feeling against him on the estate but the suggestion was firmly rejected. Other applications were also refused until he was finally offered the option of a bail hostel but it was outside the Dewsbury area and he ended up staying in Armley instead.

Karen, Craig and Michael were all in pretty much the same situation during that wet miserable summer of 2008:

alone, behind bars and scared. And all they could do was wait – wait to find out how much longer their prison lives would last.

On 5 September, at a pre-trial hearing, there was a new blow for Karen. She was also to be charged jointly with Michael Donovan with kidnapping and false imprisonment. If found guilty, she was looking at many more summers – and winters – behind bars.

18

CRAIG ON TRIAL

It was the day before Shannon Matthews' tenth birthday when Craig Meehan stepped into the dock at Dewsbury Magistrates Court. The previous year, there had been a birthday cake with pink candles for the little girl – the country knew that because they had seen the pictures of the seemingly happy occasion, released during her abduction.

This year things were very different. Her mum Karen was behind bars and the man she had called 'Dad' was on trial for viewing child pornography on the computer that had sat in the front room at 24 Moorside Road.

Rather than the traditional bench of three local magistrates, Craig's case was presided over by District Judge Jonathan Bennett. He faced 11 counts of possession of indecent images of children. Prosecutor David Holderness told the court how Craig was accused of possessing 134 indecent images of children – 133 on his computer and one on his phone. The incidents were alleged to have taken place between September 2006 and the day after Shannon went missing when the computer was seized. Craig denied everything, staring blankly ahead with his familiar gormless expression throughout the case.

As the trial began, it provided a glimpse into Craig's depraved secret life – but also into the goings-on at 24 Moorside Road which until that point had only been guessed at by the outside world. Again, the public gallery was packed. Sat among the Dewsbury Moor locals and other fascinated on-lookers was Leon Rose – Shannon's natural father and the man who had backed Craig when slurs were made against him during his daughter's disappearance.

The court was told officers had found a pile of adult sex videos when they searched the couple's home for clues in the wake of Shannon's disappearance. The find immediately disproved Craig's claims during police interviews he had never used any kind of pornography. It was only later he admitted to police that he had viewed adult porn.

Mr Holderness spoke quietly and soberly as he told the courtroom that police computer experts who examined Meehan's computer had found that search words including 'rape', 'incest' and 'daughter' had been used. The key plank of Craig's defence was that 24 Moorside Road had been very much an open house, with dozens of people coming and going – and any one of them could have logged on to his computer to download child porn.

His cousins Damian and Ryan Meehan gave evidence that they were often at the house from 9.00am in the morning until 10.00pm at night – although they claimed they had never seen any child pornography on the computer. But records of Meehan's work shifts were presented to the court showing that all the downloading of child pornography had taken place while he was not at work.

'The number of downloads when he was not at work made it extremely unlikely that someone else accessed his house and computer to carry out the downloads in question,' said Mr Holderness. In fact, one of the first downloads of child porn had taken place at 7.28am on the morning after the computer had been bought second-hand. It seemed highly unlikely that anyone else could have been in the house at that time of day.

Mr Holderness also said police had found the password 'Reggie07' had been used to protect the computer – which Craig accepted was his nickname. Craig had claimed that he found child pornography sites 'disgusting' and wouldn't go on them but said he had accidentally stumbled upon some while searching the internet for songs. But Det Con Andrew James, from West Yorkshire Police's Hi-tech crime unit, said, 'Looking at the [search] results, if someone was searching for music, you would be more likely to see a group of music files together.'

Det Con James also explained to the court that 'Lolita' – a reference found 653 times on Craig's computer – was frequently used by those searching for child porn. On the second day of the trial, Craig himself stood in the witness box. On questioning he told how he was shocked when police told him about the indecent images of children on his computer. He said he had no idea what the word 'Lolita' meant and certainly no clue how to spell it.

During questioning, he began to cast light on the workings of his relationship with Karen – and how he had walked out on her more than six times. 'We had a pretty good relationship,' he said quietly. 'But there were times when we argued, she said I was cheating on her. When I came home [from work] I was quite tired and just wanted to go to bed. She said I had somebody at work and was cheating on her.'

'Was there any basis for that?' Craig was asked by his barrister David Orbaum.

'No,' Craig replied.

To the shock of many in the public gallery, Craig also told the court he was still in love with Karen. All despite her having dumped him and then insisting that he and his family were behind the plot to kidnap Shannon. The admission came as Mr Orbaum asked him how he thought the images might have got on to his computer.

'It could have been done by accident, it could have been done on purpose. I did know there were a few people trying to split me and Karen up.' He added that one person had even registered Karen on a dating website. 'A few people knew the password so they could have just turned it on,' he said. 'It were generally access to anybody,' he said.

Then when Mr Orbaum suggested child porn was only a small step up from adult porn, Craig replied, 'The thing is, there were no need for me to do that. I don't like it. I'm in a relationship, or I was, with someone I still do love, who was ten years older than me.'

He claimed he would never have risked that relationship by looking at child pornography. 'I've got more to lose to look at child porn that I have anything else and I wouldn't want to throw a four-year relationship away with something as ridiculous as that,' he told the packed courtroom.

Craig was back in the dock on 16 September, preparing to hear his verdict. Again, he was wearing his black Man U

'Ronaldo' shirt. There were mutterings in the public gallery about how frequently, or not, the shirt might have been washed. Craig had never smelled fresh at the best of times.

District Judge Bennett's judgment went on for ten pages. It must quickly have become apparent to Craig that he was being found guilty. But when he finally heard the words – that he had been found guilty of 11 counts of possessing 49 indecent images of children – his expression remained utterly blank, refusing to give away any indication of the inner horror he must have been feeling. But Craig's lack of emotion was compensated for by his sister Amanda Hyett who broken down in racking sobs at the back of the court. On the scale of indecent pictures of children, six images were at level four, two at level three, ten at level two and 31 at level one – with level five being the most serious. He was cleared on the count of possessing an image on a mobile phone.

District Judge Jonathan Bennett told Craig they were 'serious matters'. 'The damage that has been caused to the children in these photographs is unimaginable,' he said, knowing his words would be appearing in every one of the next day's newspapers. 'That is why Parliament regards these matters as so serious and why there is widespread social abhorrence of such offences. The most vulnerable in our society have to be protected.'

Craig was sentenced to 20 weeks in prison, made subject to a seven-year sexual offences prevention order banning him from having photographs of children under 16 unless it was with permission of the child's parents and prohibited from viewing any image of children, except for family photos.

Because Craig had already served 166 days on remand,

he was free to go immediately. But Judge Bennett knew that even outside prison Craig's life would remain in many ways like a jail. He said Craig had become 'almost a household figure' as a result of the publicity surrounding Shannon's disappearance. 'The conviction for these offences will be further publicised,' he said. 'Such cases often attract publicity, but your case – as is demonstrated by the enormous media attention – will be far more than most. Undoubtedly as a result of the events of this year your life has changed forever. Life cannot go back to what it was before 19 February. Over the coming months you are going to face some difficult circumstances.'

Judge Bennett could not have been more right. The most immediate difficulty for Craig was where he should go next. A clear sign was being sent out by the people of Dewsbury Moor: 'We don't want you back.' There was talk of lynching and beatings should he return, and Craig's family knew the neighbours well enough to know they were serious. Even Dewsbury Moor's voice of reason, Julie Bushby, sent out a strong message to Craig, saying the estate was disgusted and disappointed with what he had done.

'If he comes back up to the Moor, I don't think he'll get very far,' she said. 'He won't be able to go back.' Julie said he deserved the verdict he had received. 'At the end of the day, what he's done was wrong,' she said. 'How can I describe it? It's sick; end of.'

Craig was whisked away from the court hidden beneath a police jacket in the back of an unmarked car. By his side sat his mother, Alice. The car was flanked by two marked cars with sirens blaring and lights flashing. The police were keen to get Craig away at the earliest opportunity before there was a chance for those angered by his crimes to take affairs into their own hands.

Alice Meehan and his sister Amanda Hyett were both standing by Craig. 'He's only my brother, he's my blood, I didn't choose him to do that,' Amanda said after leaving the court in tears.

Craig was sacked by Morrisons following the conviction and was now jobless and homeless, and the woman he said he loved was facing the likelihood of a lengthy jail stretch.

Just one week after sentencing, Craig Meehan was in a very bad way. It emerged that he had attempted suicide more than once and only his mother had been able to talk him out of it. Alice Meehan told the *Yorkshire Evening Post*, 'He was very low when I spoke to him on Saturday, he was thinking about doing something stupid. Everything is going around in his head.'

Alice explained Craig really was still in love with Karen and finding their separation hard to deal with. He was also still struggling to come to terms with his father's death the previous November. Craig's vulnerable state only worsened when he was identified by a gang of teenage boys and beaten up in the street.

Afterwards, the police installed an alarm and high-tech video surveillance equipment at his new address and carried out extra patrols outside his home. Officers even told him to alert his local police station every time he went out and offered to do his shopping to keep him out of public sight. But that only made Craig feel even more ostracised.

Soon after the street beating, Craig disappeared after a boozy night at his safe house where he downed can after can of strong lager and cider. The following morning, he went to pick up his income support from a post office –

then simply disappeared. Friends and family feared the worst. Alice alerted police that her son was missing. How ironic that call was coming just seven months after Karen Matthews's initial 999 call about her own missing child which had set the whole chain of events in motion.

'Craig's in a really bad way and we are desperately worried for his safety. He normally lets his mum and sister know what he's up to but they've not heard a thing,' said one relative. 'Craig's been talking about trying to visit Shannon's real father Leon Rose to find out where she is. He's also mumbling about fighting a custody battle for her, so his head is all over the place. The police won't tell us anything. We are really worried.'

Craig eventually returned to the safe house where he stayed in hiding. But he remained angry about his conviction, and still fiercely declaring his innocence he launched an appeal. In January 2009, at Leeds Crown Court, Judge Geoffrey Marson QC allowed the appeal against two of the images – one from a level-one image and the other a level three. David Orbaum, again representing Craig, said the prosecution was offering no evidence on the two images due to an agreed basis of facts.

Mr Orbaum said, 'The appellant accepts he searched the internet for, and then downloaded, adult pornography on to his computer. As a consequence of these searches, indecent images of children were downloaded, all of which were deleted.' Judge Marson then quashed Craig's conviction against the two counts. Afterwards, Craig abandoned his appeal against the other charges.

For a couple of months after his own conviction, Craig

was able to slip out of the spotlight. But, with Karen and Michael's trial about to start at the beginning of November, the climax of the drama around little Shannon Matthews was still to come.

19

THE TRIAL

Leeds City Centre was buzzing with excitement. Television broadcasting vans lined the street outside the Crown Court for more than 200 yards and the courtroom vestibules and barristers' rooms were packed with defence and prosecution legal teams scurrying around carrying huge files of documents and papers.

Journalists from virtually every national newspaper were there, fighting for the best places in the press box. Those with less sharp elbows ended up watching events from an overspill room set up next door with a videolink. The public gallery in Courtroom 12 was filled with many of the residents of Dewsbury Moor who had experienced and observed the drama of the past nine months.

It was Tuesday, 11 November – the first day of one of the biggest trials the court had ever seen. From the very beginning, the case of Shannon Matthews had attracted national press attention. But there was another reason for so much interest in the trial because absolutely no one was sure how it was going to play out. Normally, on the really big trials, everyone is pretty certain of the verdict before the jury is even sworn in. But in this case, with so many claims and counter-claims being made by Michael Donovan and Karen Matthews, nothing about what was to unfold could be certain.

At 2.00pm, the court was settled and a silent anticipation swept the room as a clink of a key chain heralded the arrival of Karen Matthews and Michael Donovan from the cells. The pair emerged together, just one security guard separating them. But, despite their physical closeness again, they could have been in different worlds. They didn't even exchange a glance and each seemed oblivious of the other's presence.

Karen had piled on weight while in prison and her pale face now looked pudgy and drooping. But she seemed quite relaxed and even smiled warmly when handed a cup of water before procedures got under way. Michael, meanwhile, dressed in a dark sweatshirt and jogging bottoms, looked more gaunt than ever, his hair thin and his bones jutting out above the hollows of his cheeks. His eyes were still bulging and stared fixedly at a point in the distance. He stooped forwards in the dock, making him appear a good few inches shorter than his actual 5ft 8ins.

The pair had been placed behind a sheet of plastic fixed to the dock and designed to prevent any chance of escape, but it created the impression that they were two contrasting exhibits in a museum. To Michael's side sat a helper who had been designated by the court to explain any events or issues that took place which he might not understand. The mere attendance of the 'appropriate adult' gave a huge indication of just how helpless and hopeless Donovan was thought to be.

The jury of seven men and five women were then sworn in. Many of the jurors looked slightly overawed as they glanced across to the dock and instantly realised what a high-profile case they had been selected for.

The trial began in earnest the following morning as the charges were read out. The pair were both charged with kidnap and false imprisonment of Shannon Matthews, in addition to perverting the course of justice. Prosecutor Julian Goose QC began his opening address to the jury, saying the 'overwhelming likelihood is that the reason for the plan was dishonestly to obtain the reward money offered by the press'.

His words immediately revealed the prosecution were giving no truck to Karen's excuses that Shannon's disappearance had started off as a white lie to Craig which had got out of all control. Mr Goose continued, 'Karen Matthews made impassioned public pleas for the recovery of her daughter, some of those you will see from television recordings shown on national television. Karen Matthews also gave deliberately misleading and false leads for investigation by the police.'

He went on to detail Michael's part in the plot – that he had kept Shannon 'drugged, subdued and hidden from the public', buying newspapers to keep abreast of the mounting reward money. Mr Goose also mentioned the friends and neighbours on the Dewsbury Moor estate – many of whom were now squashed in the public gallery – who had worked so hard to find Shannon, 'only then to discover that it had all been a lie, a trick and deliberately false complaint'.

Karen Matthews's initial 999 call to report Shannon missing was then played to the courtroom. As the tape began, Karen's broad Yorkshire accent seemed to bounce off every wall. She looked impassively ahead, like a stroppy teenager who has just been grounded, as she heard her own words, her own lies, being retold to the world. Her entire body language seemed to scream that teenage mantra: 'It's not fair!'

Mr Goose seemed almost impressed by Karen's acting abilities. 'The prosecution say that Karen Matthews is a consummate and convincing liar,' he said. He then explained how Karen and Michael had intended to get away with their far-fetched plot, revealing Michael had told the police during interviews, 'The plan was to release Shannon in Dewsbury Market and for Michael to discover her. The plan thereafter was to claim the reward which, by the time of Shannon's discovery, was £50,000.'

Mr Goose then went into the often-quoted statistics of the mammoth search for Shannon – how it cost £3.2 million, used more than 300 officers and 75 per cent of Britain's specialist dogs, searched 1,800 premises and analysed 800 CCTV tapes. In addition, there were 41 searches made further afield, including some as far away as Cumbria and Nottinghamshire.

The jury was then played some of the televised appeals which Karen had made during Shannon's disappearance. Karen refused to look at the screen which beamed her face to the court and instead continued to stare straight ahead. Mr Goose then revealed to the jury something of what Shannon's life had been like for the 24 days she was incarcerated at Lidgate Gardens. He talked about the list of rules left on top of the television set, concluding with the chilling threat 'IPU' – 'I Promise You'.

And he explained how urine tests on Shannon following

her release showed she had been given the sedative Temazepam and a cocktail of other drugs to 'quieten and subdue' her. This was a new and particularly shocking revelation for many in the courtroom and there was an audible gasp from the public gallery.

A description of the elasticated strap tied to a roof beam which was used to restrain Shannon was equally shocking for those listening. Mr Goose then went on to explain the claims and counter-claims that Karen and Michael had made against each other in a series of contradictory and conflicting police interviews. It must have left many of the jurors wondering what on earth they were in for as the case unfolded.

The prosecutor continued by describing how Michael claimed that Karen had planned the abduction in a bid to earn money, but that he had acted under duress in fear for his life. But Mr Goose said the prosecution rejected Michael's excuses. 'He was a willing participant in a plan agreed with Karen Matthews,' he said.

Karen, meanwhile, had been blaming anyone she could think of in her police interviews including Craig, his mother and his sister Amanda. In some interviews, she said she knew Michael was keeping Shannon overnight but in another statement she claimed not to have had any idea where her daughter was during her disappearance. Mr Goose cut to the chase: 'The prosecution say that Karen Matthews tells us lies to suit her purpose and can't be believed in this trial.'

One of the first witness statements read to the court was by Michael's sister, Maria Harper. Her account told how her brother had told stories and fantasised from a very young age. Detective Superintendent Andy Brennan, the senior investigating officer in the search for Shannon, then explained to the court quite how massive the search had been – and what a huge toll it had placed on the force's resources. He explained that, at one point, between 75 and 85 detectives were working on the inquiry, compared with between 10 and 15 in a murder inquiry. As a result, officers had been pulled off other serious murder and rape cases.

But Det Supt Brennan said he had never had any doubt that he was dealing with a genuine missing-person inquiry. 'It was quite unlike anything I've been involved with,' he said.

The following morning, Julie Bushby entered the witness box. Despite the awfulness of Shannon's disappearance and Karen's involvement, she said she remained fiercely proud of everything the residents of Dewsbury Moor had achieved during the hunt. Julie was followed by Natalie Brown who'd put a roof over Karen and her family's head in the early days of Shannon's disappearance.

Natalie's evidence was hugely damning of her friend. When asked to compare Karen's moods when the police were there and when they were not, she said simply, 'It was like Jekyll and Hyde.' She also recounted the conversation she heard Karen having at the Community House about a young police officer when she'd said 'she wouldn't mind taking him upstairs'. And, when asked if she ever saw Karen cry, Natalie answered, 'I never saw any real tears coming from Karen; her eyes would well up but that was it.'

Equally unhelpful to Michael was evidence from his niece Caroline Meehan. When asked by Mrs Frances Oldham, QC, appearing on behalf of Karen, if she agreed that her uncle was 'a loner, a strange character, a bit creepy and a fantasist', Caroline simply replied, 'Yes.'

Mrs Oldham sought to muddy the waters surrounding the Meehan family at this point by referring back to the time that Caroline had been arrested with her mother and sisters on a charge of perverting the course of justice. Even though the women had been released without charge, Mrs Oldham asked Caroline what the police had questioned her on after her arrest.

She claimed that, using mobile phone records, detectives had established that Caroline Meehan had rung her mum just after 5.40pm on 14 March, the day Shannon Matthews was found. She went on, 'The police asked you whether during that conversation Alice Meehan had said, "Don't worry, they will never find out. Don't worry, as long as you keep your mouth shut."'

Ms Meehan agreed the police had asked her about that but she had told them her mum had never said those words to her. 'Did you know anything that would have required you to keep your mouth shut?' asked Mrs Oldham.

'No,' Ms Meehan replied.

Mrs Oldham then asked, 'Did you know anything about your brother, Craig, your sister, Amanda, or her husband, Neil?'

But Caroline Meehan firmly denied knowing of any involvement of any members of her family in the plot.

It must have been a welcome relief to jurors as the first week of the trial came to an end, and Karen and Michael must have been equally pleased to have two days away from the intense atmosphere of the courtroom. But Armley Jail was no place of respite for Michael. He had already been threatened by other inmates and his prison identity card had mysteriously disappeared.

There were doubts Michael would even make it to Leeds

Crown Court that Friday after he had been punched twice in the face the previous evening in jail. Inmates reading about the trial in newspapers and watching television reports in which the elasticated strap were mentioned were clearly unhappy about what he was accused of doing.

Michael was left with a red mark beneath his nose; he was finding it painful to talk and could only eat soup or pureed food through a straw. He was unable to put in his false teeth, so in court his face looked even more emaciated and caved in than usual.

Back in court on the following Monday, Michael's legal team told the judge they were still concerned about his health. He hadn't eaten properly for three days and was still in extreme pain. The day's sitting was adjourned to enable him to receive further medical attention during which X-rays showed he had actually suffered a double fractured jaw.

By the Tuesday, the court sitting was back on schedule and the jury were shown a television montage of Karen Matthews's TV appeals. Shot after shot flashed up on a screen showing Karen, red-eyed, brimming with tears, pleading and begging for Shannon to come home or for whoever was holding her to let her go.

This was followed by readings of Karen's interviews with police both before and after her arrest. A transcript of the interview she gave after Michael Donovan's arrest – in which she denied any knowledge at all of Shannon being with him – was read out slowly by Det Con John Lee.

Next up, forensic toxicologist Dr Chatterton told the court that traces of the mildly 'potent hypnotic' drug Temazepam and the travel-sickness medication Melcozine, which causes mild drowsiness, were found in Shannon's urine after she was discovered – suggesting she had taken them at some point in the past 72 hours. He also revealed that a hair sample showed the drugs had been taken for as long as 20 months. Traces of the drug were found in all 20cm of the length of hair tested.

Day six of the trial – 20 November – proved to be one of the most daunting days in court for the jurors when they were shown the long, white elastic strap with a noose on one end which had been used to tether Shannon at Lidgate Gardens. The 12 jury members watched intently as the strap was unrolled before them by scene-of-crime officer Frances Senior.

Then it was time for the court to hear how Michael had attempted to cast blame on Karen during his interviews with police at Halifax Police Station following his arrest. The court was read the prepared statement he had given to officers, in which he claimed Karen had threatened to set three men on him if he didn't help her, how he'd picked Shannon up that bitter and foggy February evening and promised to take her to the fair then driven her back to his Batley Carr flat.

Then transcripts were read out of interviews with Karen after she was arrested, by which time her story had changed considerably. By now, she was saying she knew Michael had Shannon but thought he'd only keep her for a day while she worked out how to leave Craig. 'It just went pear-shaped,' she had said. 'It didn't go to plan.' But in other interviews, read out in court the next day, she started laying the blame at Craig's door, saying he had 'planned this so I would appear to be an unfit mother'.

With the interviews being read one after the other, it was clear to the jury how far and how quickly Karen's story had changed as she sought to build the picture of herself as a victim in the plot.

On Monday, 24 November, there was another interruption to the trial when the court was unable to sit because Michael was recovering from surgery he had undertaken two days previously to fit metal plates to hold together his fractured jaw.

Mr Justice McCombe told the jury that the accused was in a 'rather bad way' but the following day he was back in court, this time making his debut in the witness box. Michael's barrister, Alan Conrad QC, opened questioning by asking his client how he felt about Karen Matthews, clearly trying to create the picture that this was a nervous, frail man terrified by the brutish woman now glaring straight ahead in the dock.

'How do you feel towards Karen? Do you like her?' Mr Conrad asked.

'No,' Michael replied.

Asked why, he went on, 'I'm scared of her. She kept threatening me.'

Certainly, Michael created the impression of a man who was timid and easily manipulated. He seemed to almost shrink inside his navy-blue jumper and jeans as questioning began. Judge Mr Justice McCombe and the defence QC repeatedly had to ask him to speak louder, even after a microphone was propped up in front of him on top of a stack of law books and the Bible.

Michael answered questions about his childhood, previous convictions, the van crash which left him seriously injured and his marriage to Susan Bird. 'She was right violent towards me. She tried to control me,' Michael told the jury about his ex, all adding to the impression that he had long been a victim at the hands of women. He then explained about the drugs he took for his various medical conditions, but he denied ever taking heroin.

Leaning on the side of the witness box for support, he then answered questions about the meeting with Karen in the café and how she'd passed him a piece of paper telling him what to do when the reward money hit £50,000. He said the instructions told him to abandon Shannon in Dewsbury market, make a pretence of 'finding' her, and then take her to the police station.

Asked how Shannon had coped with the three weeks she stayed with him, Michael replied, 'She was happy going. She always wanted to watch DVDs, play games, on the computer and stuff like that.' He said she enjoyed Disney films and her favourite Bratz toys, and he had bought her dresses, leggings, socks and shoes, using cash from his incapacity benefits. 'She said I was more better when I bought things for her,' he said.

Michael also told of the trips he had taken her on to parks in Batley and Birstall so she wouldn't be cooped up all the time and how she 'ran straight towards the swings and started playing'. Quizzed about the traces of drugs found in her body, Michael claimed Shannon suffered from travel sickness, and a pharmacist had told him to give her two of the Traveleeze tablets in the morning before breakfast to ease her condition.

But when Mr Conrad said the real reason had been suggested as to make her more compliant and drowsy, Michael responded, 'No, it's not true, that.' He totally denied ever giving Shannon Temazepam and claimed she must have stood on a chair and reached his own supply in the kitchen cupboard. When asked about the strap, he denied ever having tethered the girl.

Michael then went on to claim that, in the full 24 days Shannon stayed with him, her mother called just twice. The second time was in the second week of her disappearance. He claimed he tried to get her to speak to her daughter but Karen wasn't interested, simply saying, 'Stick to the plan.'

Michael said after Shannon had been with him for a fortnight he received a text message from an unknown sender, whom he presumed to be Karen Matthews, which told him the reward to find Shannon had reached £50,000. He then described the final moments before his capture by the police – and how he had just been making Shannon a drink when he saw officers approaching his flat.

He said, 'I told Shannon, "The police are here." She said, "Oh no, I don't want the police."' He said he started to panic and both of them ran off separately towards the back bedroom where Shannon had been sleeping. He denied that the large amount of money found in his wallet was an escape fund to take Shannon to Blackpool and also rejected claims that he'd made her wear his daughter's clothes. 'I showed her some. It was up to her if she wore it or not,' he told the jury.

On the following day, 26 November, jurors were shown a montage of CCTV footage of Michael out and about in Batley and Dewsbury. There was a trip to Boots in Dewsbury on 22 February, then visits to Asda and Tesco in the following days, and even an appointment at Dewsbury Health Centre on 6 March. Prosecutor Julian Goose asked the jury to compare the impression of a frail, helpless man that they were being shown in the dock with the tall, upright and sprightly character who appeared on the CCTV footage.

Under cross-examination by Karen's barrister, Frances

Oldham QC, Michael denied his sister Alice Meehan and Amanda Hyett had been involved in the plot. But he said he wasn't sure whether Craig Meehan had been or not. But he rejected Mrs Oldham's assertions that he had been in control of the plan and said he remained frightened of Karen throughout.

During her cross-examination, Mrs Oldham pushed the idea that Shannon's abduction had been a Meehan/Donovan family plot. She also painted a picture of Michael as a man so traumatised by the loss of his daughters in the custody battle that he might have been capable of anything.

She asked why Shannon had written letters to Donovan's daughter. 'She was bored,' Michael replied. 'She would ask me about my own children and said, "Could I write to her?" and started writing it down.'

Then he was questioned on why he had told a pharmacist on the day before Shannon's release that he was going to Blackpool for the weekend. Michael denied it.

The court then heard that while staying at his flat Shannon had drawn a picture of Blackpool – Donovan's favourite town and the place where he had gone on the run with his daughter. Shannon had also written a letter, saying, 'Dear John, when me and my dad go to Blackpool, we're going to take some pictures of Blackpool seaside and a bus. I love you, I will miss you, so will my dad. Love Shannon and Dad.' Confusingly, Michael claimed Shannon was referring to Craig Meehan when she wrote 'Dad' and said he did not know who John was. It must have seemed very confusing for the jury desperately trying to make sense of what had gone on.

Next into the box were two expert psychologist witnesses who tried to explain just how much Michael was mentally capable – or incapable – of actually doing. Dr David Glasgow told the court Michael was of limited intelligence with serious emotional issues. He said psychometric tests had shown him to have memory problems, a long history of depression and an IQ so low that he was on the borderline between learning difficulties and a more severe learning disability. Dr Glasgow said when Donovan underwent questioning his answers were 'impoverished'. He also described him as 'timid' and 'highly vulnerable' to being influenced by other people, putting his own wishes behind theirs.

Forensic psychologist Dr Harry Wood said that after interviewing Donovan he was astonished he had managed to pass a driving test. But Dr Wood said he did believe Donovan would have been able to resist a threat. Much of the case against Michael was to rest upon what he was capable of doing.

Next to enter the witness box was the 'main attraction' – Karen Matthews – whose case also focused on what she was capable of doing. But in her case it wasn't what she was physically capable of that was the issue. It was just how much cruelty this mother was capable of inflicting on her own child.

20
GUILTY

It was a chill, early winter's morning on Day 12 of the trial – 27 November – when events reached a climax. All the police evidence, expert witnesses and neighbours' testimonies had really been just a preamble to the main event – Karen Matthews entering the witness box.

Karen was under no obligation to give evidence during the trial and many thought she wouldn't put herself up for potentially being ripped to shreds by one of the country's leading prosecutors. But still stroppily defiant that none of it was her fault, she was determined that her voice be heard.

As she placed her large hand on the Bible, her hair swung down like a veil across her face. Her barrister Frances Oldham called upon the jury to judge her on the facts alone. 'The media has decided that Karen Matthews is guilty, the police have decided that Karen Matthews is guilty,' said Mrs Oldham, claiming Karen had been demonised before ever having the chance to explain herself.

Her client, making an attempt to look smart in a stone-coloured jacket, had barely been in the box two minutes when the tears started to fall. The rest of her evidence was accompanied by sobbing as she played the role of victim once again. She was handed a box of tissues which she used to wipe her tear-sodden face throughout questioning.

When asked by her barrister whether she'd had anything to do with the plot to kidnap Shannon, she acted appalled: 'I'm just disgusted because I haven't had nothing to do with it.' She claimed that, when she was told where Shannon had been, she was 'shocked'.

Karen was then asked questions to paint a picture of domestic life at 24 Moorside Road. She told how, after the birth of her youngest child, Craig had become 'violent, abusive and aggressive towards her' calling her things like 'fat and ugly'.

'He used to punch and kick me, things like that,' she said. She claimed that Craig would shout and swear at the children, mainly when drunk, although not to Shannon. She didn't explain why Shannon was treated differently but she said her daughter had always received good school reports. Karen then told the story of going to Alice Meehan's house after the row with Craig at his dad's funeral and how she had got talking to Michael while she was there. Craig has always vigorously denied that he was violent towards Karen or her children.

'He asked me if I would like to go back to his place and I refused,' Karen told the jury. 'I needed to sort my problems out with Craig.' Asked what Michael's response to her refusal had been, she said, 'It was the way he looked. He looked disgusted because I didn't take up his offer.'

Then there was a string of denials from Karen on a range

of issues: no, she'd never given her daughter Temazepam; no, she had never been to Michael's house in Lidgate Gardens; no, she had never told Michael to pick Shannon up after school; and no, she had never threatened to have him killed or his car burned out if he refused to help her.

Karen's initial 999 call was then played to the jury again, followed by her first television appeal. When asked if she had been acting all the time, Karen could barely speak for tears. 'No,' she finally said. She then admitted lying to the police in an interview on 18 March – before her arrest – when she told detectives she had never considered leaving Meehan. She said, despite wanting to leave Craig, she was too scared to do it. 'He told me if I left him he would tell people I was an unfit mother and have my children taken away from me,' she said.

Mrs Oldham then asked, 'Had Craig said anything to you about what you should say or do?'

Karen replied, 'For me to take the blame for Shannon.'

Mrs Oldham said, 'Did he say why?'

'I had no convictions and I was female and I'd get off lightly.'

Karen then told how she had become suspicious something might be going on when Craig and Amanda Hyett seemed to be having so many secret conversations during the period Shannon was missing, particularly when previously they hadn't been that close. 'When I asked them what they were talking about, none of them would tell me,' she said. 'I feel all three of them hatched the plan – kept me in the dark.'

It was also revealed that, during an interview with the police, Karen claimed Amanda Hyett was involved and told her 'to keep it hush hush' and how much money they could make to go on holiday and other things. But, in cross-examination, Michael's barrister Alan Conrad dismissed Karen's outlandish claims and accused her of more acting – this time for the jury.

'You're putting on, for the jury today, a staged performance,' Mr Conrad said. 'Just as it was a staged performance during the three-and-a-half weeks your daughter was missing.'

There was little difference in routine in Karen's second day in the witness box. Again, within minutes she was in floods of tears and continued to deny virtually everything put to her. Mr Conrad opened his morning's cross-examination with a sharp blow. 'You're telling blatant lies to this jury, aren't you?' he said.

'No,' sobbed Karen in response.

But as he reminded the jury about details from Karen's police interviews – at odds with the story she was now peddling in the box – she found herself tied in knots. She fluffed her lines, contradicted her story and sometimes simply refused to answer, as if totally confused by what she had said in the past and unable to find any other plausible – or even implausible – excuses.

Asked why she had told the police at one point that she had asked Michael to pick Shannon up from school, she babbled, 'I didn't ask him to pick her up from school. I was confused what I was saying.' Then she claimed she had never wanted to pose for pictures with Craig holding up posters appealing for information about missing Shannon. Asked who'd made her do it, she replied, 'Craig and the rest of his family.'

Mr Conrad then questioned her on the shopping expedition to buy a sat-nav and groceries on the very night

Shannon went missing. Again Karen had someone to blame – this time it was Amanda Hyett. Even more extraordinarily, she then tried to claim she had never admitted anything at all about being involved in the plot to Dec Con Christine Freeman, Natalie Brown and Julie Bushby on the night she was arrested in Batley town centre.

'I didn't say anything like that to them,' she said, despite having heard all three give evidence to the contrary just days earlier.

As the day wore on, black tear tracks ran down Karen's face from the mascara she had painted on to impress the jury. Her nose ran and she had to be handed a new box of tissues to cope with her constant stream of sobs. In a last-ditch attempt to defend herself, Karen declared, 'I love my kids to bits.'

Prosecutor Julian Goose responded, 'It's only Shannon that you seemed to try to get rid of? It's only Shannon you used in this wicked deception?'

'I didn't use her,' Karen responded through her sobs.

Mr Goose then asked her why she was crying.

'Because I'm getting blamed for something I haven't done,' came the reply.

Such was Karen's distress that, had she not spent two days contradicting herself and directing blame at everyone other than herself, there must surely have been some sense of sympathy for her in the courtroom. Instead, as she left the witness box and returned to the dock, there was just a profound sense of relief that no one was going to have to endure any more of Karen's confused lies.

All over Leeds the Christmas lights and decorations were being strung up as the trial of Karen Matthews and

Michael Donovan drew to a close at the start of December. All that remained were the barristers' closing speeches and the judge's summing up to the jury.

In his closing speech, Prosecutor Julian Goose took full advantage of Karen's pitiful performance in the witness box. 'She has lied and lied and lied again,' he said. 'To the police, various friends and you in this court. She has lied so often and so much that she has reached the point where all she can say is "I was confused" and then blame everybody else except herself.

'You may think, ladies and gentleman, and you can be sure about it, she has been found out for the dishonest and, we say, wicked liar that she is. Ladies and gentlemen, this was a plan between Karen Matthews and Michael Donovan. It was a plan to take Shannon and keep her captive and make a false complaint, wait for the reward money to grow, pretend to find her and then claim the money. That was the plan between them.'

In her closing speech, Frances Oldham took her time and seemed to almost address each juror individually as she labelled the prosecution as 'fatally flawed'. And she raised the issue that had been foremost in so many minds – just why hadn't Shannon been called as a witness?

The reality was that Shannon's statements had been so confused in parts, with some elements possibly hallucinated, that they would have been torn to shreds by the defence counsel. But Mrs Oldham's words must surely have left questions lingering in the jury members' minds: 'You have not heard from the principal witness in this case, Shannon Matthews herself. The one person who can say if she went willingly and without force or favour, or unwillingly, pushed by Donovan into the back of the car, is Shannon Matthews.'

Mrs Oldham reiterated that there was no forensic evidence – DNA or fingerprints – linking Karen to Lidgate Gardens and that many important questions had not been fully answered during the trial which she claimed left sufficient doubt about Karen's involvement.

Then – on Day 14 of the trial – it was time for the judge's summing up. Mr Justice McCombe told the seven men and five women of the jury he wanted a unanimous verdict.

The jury retired the following day to begin the discussion and debate which would lead them to verdicts on each of the three charges for the two defendants.

It was just starting to sleet outside – a return to the bitterly cold weather conditions which had first accompanied the hunt for Shannon when she went missing ten months earlier. In the end, it didn't take the jury particularly long to assess the evidence and return with verdicts. It was just over a day later when they returned to Court No 12 at about a quarter to one on 4 December.

Karen and Michael were recalled to the box, again just yards apart, although it could have been miles, such was their obvious disgust and dislike for each other. The public gallery was again packed with regulars from the Moor and other spectators enticed by the event. The press box was also bursting with journalists, pens poised and mobile phones at the ready to dash out of court and ring in a verdict to their news desks.

At the back of the court sat family liaison officers Alex Grummitt and Christine Freeman who had spent so much time with Karen. Also with them was Det Supt Brennan – the man who had overseen the inquiry and who must have felt a conviction was crucial.

The clerk of the court read out all of the charges

individually, first for Michael Donovan and then for Karen Matthews. Each time the foreman of the jury, a serious-looking young man in his mid-thirties, replied quietly but confidently, 'Guilty.'

Neither Karen nor Michael showed the merest emotion. As gasps could be heard from the public gallery and rapid scribbling from the press box, in the dock there was no reaction at all. Michael simply looked down, while Karen continued to stare straight ahead. For weeks and months, throughout her daughter's supposed disappearance and throughout her trial, Karen Matthews had been a melting pot of emotion: tears, pleas, anger and desperation. But now there was nothing. She was totally blank.

And so, it was over. Karen was led from the dock, her gaze never shifting from her feet. She was then bundled from the courthouse cells into a security van and driven through the sleety, slushy roads back to New Hall Prison. Michael was taken the short stretch back to his cell at Armley. The case was concluded. All that remained was for the pair to be returned to court for sentencing after reports on them had been completed by probation officers.

But, as Karen's barrister had suggested, there were still many unanswered questions. Had Karen and Michael really cooked the whole thing up between them? Had Michael been led into it purely out of fear of Karen? And then there was the biggest question of all? Why had Karen done it? Was it really just for the cash reward or had it been an attempt to flee Craig which had gone horribly, horribly wrong?

Over the next hours and days, friends, family members,

police officers and journalists all came up with their own theories on these issues. But, with the court and public never hearing anything from Shannon herself, many unanswered questions remained – as they do to this day.

21

'Pure Evil'

The biggest question hanging in the air as the prison vans drove away and the people of Dewsbury Moor wandered slowly down to Leeds City Station for the train home was: How could she have done that to her own daughter? It was almost too much to comprehend – that a mother would sacrifice her own daughter, then lie, lie and lie again to save her own neck.

Det Supt Andy Brennan had a clear brutal assessment of Karen: 'Pure evil.' He went on, 'Karen Matthews is a manipulative individual who has demonstrated a remarkable ability to lie. It is difficult to understand what type of mother would subject her own daughter to such a wicked and evil crime.' Brennan remained convinced Karen had been motivated by greed – and the hope a substantial reward would solve all her money problems.

And he felt convinced Shannon had been cynically selected for the 'abduction' by Karen because she was the 'more photogenic' of her brothers and sister. 'The one person Shannon should have been able to rely on more than any other person was her own mother,' said Det Supt Brennan. 'Shannon has been totally betrayed by her own mother. Karen's interest and motivations throughout this have not been for Shannon or anyone else. They have been for herself and getting her hands on £50,000.'

The reaction from Karen's family was equally damning. Karen's mother, June, told reporters, 'I feel ashamed she is my daughter. She's had more help, love and support than any of my other kids but she just didn't appreciate it. What she did is horrific but at least now Shannon and the others are away from her evil.

'If Karen loved Shannon, she wouldn't have done what she did. She did it for attention and money. She was in a lot of debt. She knew from day one where our Shannon was. Why couldn't she just have told the truth instead of pointing the finger, wasting millions of pounds and worrying us all to death? I won't see Karen again. I would crack up if I saw her. It is too much for any mother to take.'

Karen's father, Gordon – who was placed on medication for stress during the case – remained furious that Karen could not only carry out such a wicked plot but also give her family so much worry while Shannon was missing. 'She's dead to me,' said Gordon. 'I never want to see her again.'

Karen's sister Julie added, 'She is unfit to be the mother of any child. Never in my wildest dreams did I suspect Karen might have anything to do with it. It just never crossed my mind. I mean, I've seen first-hand some of the things she's put her children through over the years, and some of it has been heartbreaking. But what she did with Shannon is just beyond belief.'

Karen's brother Martin was equally outraged: 'She's a disgrace – I can't believe she's my own flesh and blood.'

Shannon's natural father Leon Rose added, 'It's shocking what happened. I can't take it in.'

Clarence Mitchell, spokesman for the McCann family, who had been both the inspiration for and almost a victim of the money-making scam, said, 'It is beyond belief that anyone could have sought to exploit poor Madeleine's plight in this way.'

But not everyone was entirely convinced that Karen's motivation had been financial. Det Con Christine Freeman remained confused as to the real motive behind the crime. 'Even after spending all that time with Karen, I can't figure her out,' she said. 'I don't think she's evil. I think she's stupid, selfish, cruel and the worst mother you could imagine, but I don't think she has the intelligence to orchestrate the plan to get a reward.

'I think she agreed to go and stay with Donovan, and told him to pick up Shannon. But when she changed her mind, she reported Shannon missing to explain her absence to Craig. She could never have anticipated the scale of the media response. But that's not to say that she didn't revel in it. Either way, she kidnapped her own little girl, something unthinkable for a mother to do.'

There also remained lurking concerns in many minds that there must have also been others involved in the plot. Det Supt Brennan said, 'The case is closed,' but added, 'If new evidence comes to light it will of course be investigated. We considered all the evidence, including what Shannon said, with the Crown Prosecution Service, and concluded there was not sufficient evidence to charge anyone else.'

And, despite agreeing the evidence had clearly shown Karen's guilt, Julie Bushby remained convinced she could not have pulled off the plot alone. 'I feel sorry for Karen, I really do, because I think she is carrying the can for other people,' said Julie. 'If Karen isn't going to break and say what the full story is, what can us little people do to help her? All it takes is for someone to have one too many and then the truth comes out. I don't know who else is involved in this. I haven't got the foggiest.'

In many ways, Julie had been one of the greatest victims of the plot – having spent so much time and energy coordinating the search for a girl who wasn't even missing. But despite all that, outside court she still said she loved Karen 'to bits'.

There was condemnation for Michael Donovan too, although mostly it was tinged with a degree of pity for the man who appeared in court to be pretty inadequate at coping with life. Det Supt Brennan cautioned against too much sympathy for him though, saying, 'He's a sad and pathetic individual but he is quite clever in that he tried to maintain this persona of a dysfunctional individual incapable of making any decisions on his own. The reality is it has been a charade. He's more than capable of living a normal life.'

The Sunday after the verdict, Amanda Hyett, one of Karen's most stalwart supporters during the search, came out with a string of damning revelations in an interview with the *News of the World*.

She claimed Karen had seduced her uncle at the wake for her dad, Brian Meehan, then lured him into taking part in the plot to abduct Shannon. 'She deserves all she gets,' said Amanda. 'I hate her and my uncle Michael for what they did. They should rot in hell.

'She never loved Shannon one bit. The poor kid would be stuck in her room most of the time while she kept an open house, partying with any t*sser off the street who turned up with a tin of beer in his hand. Crate after crate of lager would go into the house. Karen would top it up with alcopops. I heard she even snorted cocaine off the living-room table.'

And she claimed Karen had revelled in her television and newspaper appearances during Shannon's disappearance. 'She loved all the attention and celebrity,' said Amanda. 'She fancied herself as the Kerry Katona of Dewsbury.'

Karen and Michael spent that Christmas behind bars unsure of how many more months and years they would be spending in jail. Sentencing was to take place on 23 January 2009. A pile of reports by probation officers about Karen's and Michael's attitude towards the crime and their mental states had been sent to the judge for consideration, and, before sentencing, the pair's barristers addressed the judge, hoping to mitigate their actions.

Speaking for Karen, Frances Oldham QC refuted the police opinion that Karen was 'pure evil'. 'She is not Myra Hindley, she's not Rose West,' Mrs Oldham insisted. Instead, she painted the picture of a woman with a pitifully low IQ – just 74 – who often behaved in a childlike manner, switching from tears to giggles in seconds, particularly when she felt anxious. She said it was that which perhaps explained the sudden personality changes during Shannon's disappearance.

She also told how a psychologist had concluded Karen did not have the 'thinking skills' necessary for such a well-planned and executed kidnap plot. Mrs Oldham then went on to say that, during seven hours of interviews with the police, Shannon had told of contact with other members of her family during her time staying with Michael – although this evidence had not been put before the jury. Even now it is unclear whether this 'contact' was something Shannon had hallucinated.

Mrs Oldham suggested the judge 'may come to the conclusion others were involved who were not before the jury, although that does not absolve Karen Matthews of her culpability'.

Alan Conrad QC, mitigating for Michael Donovan, reminded the judge of his client's medical problems and the tough time he had endured in prison because of his notoriety.

Mr Justice McCombe then began his sentencing. He told how reports presented to him had shown Karen had endured a difficult childhood, in which educational achievement 'appears to have been of little value'. She had grown up with 'inconsistent parenting, few if any social boundaries and a lack of positive role models, guidance or support'.

In the absence of expectation, the probation officer reported, 'she failed to generate personal and practical aspirations and her only ambition was to become a mother'. She had then gone on to be 'disappointed by a number of personal relationships' characterised by domestic violence, poor communication and acrimonious separations.

But the judge pulled no punches in his assessment of Karen and Michael's crime. 'The offences that you committed were truly despicable,' said Mr Justice McCombe. 'It is impossible to conceive how you could have found it in you to put this young girl through the ordeal that you inflicted upon her.

'It is incomprehensible that you could have permitted your friends, neighbours and, in your case, Matthews, even your children to sacrifice time and energy in extensive searches for the supposedly missing child.'

But the judge said he thought it 'doubtful' Karen and Michael could have planned and carried out the kidnap without the help of others because of their low intelligence. Mr Justice McCombe then talked about a report on how Shannon had been coping since the ordeal. He said it stated Shannon was 'disturbed and traumatised' afterwards, plagued with flashbacks and nightmares about being tied up.

Finally, he came to his decision on sentencing – Karen Matthews and Michael Donovan were both given concurrent sentences of six years and three years for kidnapping and false imprisonment. They were given an additional two-year sentence, to be served consecutively, for perverting the course of justice. A charge of child cruelty against Karen was ordered to lie on the file.

With time served on remand and with good behaviour by the pair, they could possibly walk free from jail in the spring of 2012.

With justice seen to be done, public anger turned away from Karen and Michael and towards someone or something else to blame for what happened. The spotlight came to rest on Social Services.

How come no one had noticed the conditions in which Karen was raising her kids? And why had no one stepped in to save Shannon before it was too late? With revelations that she had at one time been on the 'at risk' register but removed from it in 2004, attention was centred on Kirklees Council.

Friends, neighbours and Karen's sister Julie Poskitt had all made their concerns about the family known to Social

Services but felt they were either not taken seriously or that social workers were too easily duped by Karen's claims to be caring properly for her kids. Julie led the charge: 'I am furious Social Services never seemed to react to my concerns.' And former neighbour Claire Wilson said Social Services 'should be shot'.

The accusations came against a backdrop of fury about the way Social Services in Haringey, North London, had failed to step in to save 'Baby P' – the 17-month-old boy who had died at the hands of his mother and her boyfriend following a string of failings by the local Social Services.

In both the Baby P and Shannon Matthews cases, there was an outcry against Social Services for failing to safeguard children from their feckless – and sometimes evil – parents. At the end of the trial, an independent review was ordered into the way that Social Services had dealt with Shannon Matthews's family in the months and years before she was kidnapped. Kirklees local Safeguarding Children Board commissioned the independent Serious Case Review after being approached by the Department for Children, Schools and Families.

A spokesman for the council said, 'People will be rightly concerned to be reassured that professionals in the field of childcare acted properly.'

Dewsbury MP and Government Minister Shahid Malik, who called for the review, said, 'My gut instinct tells me that this is not a Baby P-type case but the truth is that we don't know what this actually is. I think the sensible thing is for Kirklees Council to initiate an independent review, which will raise public confidence and demonstrate the council has nothing to hide.'

The Shannon Matthews case also provoked a period of

general soul-searching about the lives led by hundreds of thousands of adults and children on some of Britain's forgotten council estates. Before attention focused on the case, many people simply had no idea that women like Karen Matthews existed.

Initially, she was thought to be an aberration – having seven children by six different fathers – but, when the realisation dawned on social commentators and the wider public that Karen wasn't an isolated case, it led to a mass public debate. One Tory councillor, John Ward, from Medway in Kent, said Karen was an example of 'breakdown Britain' and advocated compulsory sterilisation for parents on benefits. He was later forced to resign but the spirit of his message was repeated up and down the country, with people railing at a class of 'Vicky Pollards' – producing kids by different fathers pausing only to pocket the child benefit before moving on to the next man.

Seeing Karen Matthews sobbing on *News at Ten* brought the reality of her life and others like her into the homes of the British middle classes. The mere idea that one sector of society had been so ignorant about goings-on in another sector of the same society posed significant questions about the state of modern Britain itself.

Much analysis followed in newspapers and on television about what was actually going on in Britain's council estates. Statistics emerged showing that, while in the 1970s only 11 per cent of council tenant households weren't working, that figure had now escalated so that barely one-third of working-age tenants had full-time work.

Figures also showed that less than 15 per cent of the households were headed by a couple with children. Two-thirds were occupied by single parents. In most of these cases, according to the research, few children saw a positive father figure. With these kinds of statistics, social problems might become lined up like dominoes: depression, alcoholism, drug addiction and kids joining gangs.

For girls, often born while their mothers are still young, it could become the norm to grow up with 'guesting' fathers entering and leaving the home. They were then destined to repeat the behaviour of their mothers. And NSPCC research has shown a child growing up in such a domestic set-up was more than six times more likely to suffer abuse.

But child abuse is not purely a class issue. A report in the medical journal *The Lancet* published the day before Karen's and Michael's verdicts were announced suggested one million children in Britain were victims of abuse every year. The abuse was defined as either 'hitting with an implement, punching, beating or burning'. It also recorded at least 15 per cent of girls and 10 per cent of boys are exposed to sexual abuse – ranging from being shown pornographic material to penetrative sexual acts.

Both the Baby P and Shannon cases led to more demands for kids to be taken into care by Social Services who themselves were blamed for being too cosy with parents. But the statistics showed that in the past ten years there had already been an increase of 20 per cent in the numbers of children being taken away from their parents. And still the problems continued.

Being put into care is no golden opportunity for most youngsters – statistics also show that nearly half of all the under-21s in the criminal justice system have been in care and a huge one-third of all homeless people have been in care. All these statistics and reports coming in the wake of the Shannon trial and Baby P case required the country as a whole to do some serious thinking about its parenting.

Labour MP Frank Field, speaking about the cases, said that as a nation we are 'as a result of family breakdown of the extreme kind seen in the Matthews case, facing a social crisis in parenting every bit as dramatic as the economic recession we are now entering'. He went on to make the point that parents were no longer 'made aware by society of what is expected of them and what the community will contribute'.

Karen Matthews clearly had no idea what was expected of her as a parent. And perhaps the extraordinary thing is no one ever told her. She just continued living her life in an almost childlike fashion – doing exactly what she wanted when she wanted, and all funded by benefits. And with no one ever to curb her innate selfishness, it simply spiralled out of control until she thought nothing of abandoning her child with a man with a severely damaged history, faking an abduction and sitting back to pocket £50,000.

Some commentators blamed the welfare state, others blamed the disappearance of a sense of shame in society, and others blamed Thatcher economics for destroying manufacturing industry in the north of England and breeding a generation without hope. But those on Dewsbury Moor who saw things clearest knew really that only Karen Matthews and Michael Donovan were truly at fault.

If the case of Shannon Matthews did some good, perhaps it was to open people's eyes to the reality of lives for many children, just like Shannon, growing up with mothers, if not exactly like Karen, certainly in the same situation as Karen. But at the same time it mustn't be forgotten that the case also highlighted the phenomenal community spirit alive and well in Dewsbury Moor, also among people in similar situations to Karen Matthews.

'Look, I've got three kids from two different fathers,' said Julie Bushby, explaining the hypocrisy behind many of the attacks on Dewsbury Moor. 'Aren't some middle-class women the same? When they do it they are "having a second family". That's OK for them but not for us. People here talk to each other, help one another. Do they do that in middle-class areas? Half the time they never know the name of the person they're living next to.'

During Shannon's disappearance, Dewsbury Moor exhibited a community spirit that many people thought had long since died away in busy, modern Britain. And so it seems that in that bitter tail-end of winter, when the nation's attention turned to a small estate glued to the side of a hill outside Dewsbury, the very worst and very best of 21st-century Britain was on show to all.

22

SHANNON IS FOUND

It seems strange that so little is still known about the little girl who became the focus of one of the country's biggest missing person's inquiries and high-profile trials. There is the description of what she was wearing the day she went missing – the black school jumper and trousers – and the detail that she loved Bratz dolls and was quite 'timid' and 'shy'. But beyond that, we know hardly anything.

Karen Matthews' own descriptions of her 'little princess' during the disappearance did little to flesh out the picture of what Shannon was really like. What were her favourite subjects at school? What did she want to do when she grew up? How did she feel about her Mum's chaotic lifestyle?

Maybe Karen didn't really know herself. Maybe she had never bothered to find out. And despite hours of gentle questioning by the police, none of the evidence Shannon provided about her time with Michael was laid before the court. So again, we learned little of the freckle-faced nine-year-old and how she had coped with her ordeal.

From the moment she was rescued from Lidgate Gardens, Shannon has been cared for by the police and then Kirklees Social Services, totally shielded from the public gaze. For Shannon's long-term welfare, keeping her safe and away from the media spotlight must surely be the best thing for her. It will be hard enough growing up with the knowledge that her own mother kidnapped her, most likely with the motive of grabbing £50,000. To have to endure that in the full glare of the public eye would be horrific.

As Karen's mother June said, 'She's Karen's baby and when all's said and done Shannon will be thinking in her little mind, "Why did my mummy do that to me?" That will be in that child's mind forever – she'll never forget what they did to her.'

In the early days after Shannon's release there were reports from those working with her that she was being tormented by nightmare hallucinations and was struggling to remember members of her own family. She also complained of nightmares in which she was tied up. Some of that may have been shock and the effects of the drugs she had been fed. Since then, she has undergone child psychotherapy sessions and the reports are that she is much more settled and 'doing well'.

For the officers who worked night and day on the Shannon Matthews inquiry, life has returned to normal – with their efforts now being concentrated on the more day-to-day crimes and duties that come their way. Det Con Paul Kettlewell and Det Con Nick Townsend, who finally discovered Shannon, have retired from the force – knowing that their persistence in going the extra mile that March day may have saved a little girl's life.

The West Yorkshire Police Force emerged well from the operation. Despite initial criticisms that they could have traced Shannon quicker, the trial highlighted what a huge task that was – particularly when no one had ever mentioned the existence of Michael Donovan to them.

The force's refusal to scale down the search at any point – despite using 300 officers and 85 detectives at a cost of £3.2 million – showed a terrific commitment to finding Shannon despite all the statistics saying she was most likely dead. More than 3,000 homes were searched and 6,000 people were interviewed. It was a gargantuan effort but they were adamant that everything possible would be done to find Shannon – and her abductor.

And, coming so soon after the Madeleine McCann case, they were desperate to avoid any comparisons with the criticised Portuguese investigation into that little girl's disappearance.

A year after Shannon's disappearance, council workers spent three days clearing the house at 24 Moorside Road of its belongings so that a new family could be moved in. Almost two years on, the house looks pretty similar, its blank features giving little clue as to the machinations and deceit which went on behind its – at the time – grubby net curtains.

Council officials wrote to Karen in jail, asking her which possessions from her home she would want to keep, but she refused to take any of them, including pictures of the children now growing up without her. The pink magnolia tree planted in the front garden to celebrate Shannon's release was uprooted long ago and planted elsewhere – members of the Community Association didn't want to give vandals the opportunity to use the tree as a means of venting their anger against Karen and Craig.

Life across Dewsbury Moor has returned to normal. The estate has survived the frequent – and often unfair – attacks made on it in the media during Shannon's disappearance when it was routinely labelled a 'sink estate' and according to the *Sun* was 'like Beirut – only worse'. Then its residents were compared with the fictional characters of TV's *Shameless*, or *Emmerdale*'s the Dingles – dependent on benefits with no aspirations, education or inspiration.

As with most things, the reality was – and is – more complex. The number of people unemployed and on benefits on the Moor remains above the national average. There are some, like Karen Matthews, who spend a chunk of their benefits on cheap booze and their days watching television, smoking fags and eating chips. But these people are not peculiar to Dewsbury Moor – there are plenty of families living a very similar existence across Britain. And there are many worse estates in Britain.

In fact, Dewsbury Moor has a large number of residents who are hard-working (male unemployment is beneath 10 per cent), who take good care of their homes, mow their lawns and keep their kids under control. So it would be too easy to blame Karen Matthews's behaviour on her circumstances. Plenty of people on Dewsbury Moor have had a very similar background to hers but run their lives very, very differently.

The speed and power of the campaign set up in the wake of Shannon's disappearance also proved the hard work, enthusiasm and compassion of many of the estate's residents. And if local people can take heart from anything in this sorry saga, it is that they were roundly praised for the sense of community spirit exhibited in the hunt for the missing girl. Old, young, white, Asian, employed and unemployed all worked alongside each other hour after hour determined to do whatever possible to bring Shannon home.

'This is a good place to live,' boasted Julie Bushby. 'People want to live on here now.'

There is also optimism that the sense of community that brought together Asians and whites during the search for Shannon will remain. The estate shared one Labour and two Liberal Democrat councillors with the rest of West Dewsbury, and all of them were called Hussein. The Labour councillor, Mumtaz Hussein, said, 'I have heard so many people saying the police have done a fantastic job, which isn't a view you always get on the estates.'

The police have also announced a new blitz on anti-social behaviour locally, even though almost everyone is agreed crime and yobbishness are nowhere near what they were a few years ago.

But close friends of Karen still living on the estate have been left scarred by the way someone they felt so close to was able to dupe them so easily and with so little remorse. 'I feel like I have been punched in the stomach by someone I trusted,' recalled Petra Jamieson.

Julie Bushby agreed with the sense of betrayal felt by many on the estate. 'People felt anger, frustration, used and abused,' she said.

At the time of writing, Michael Donovan still remains at Armley Jail. In the run-up to and during the trial, he suffered extreme bullying inside prison. At one point he was even made to work as a 'slave' for another con, fetching and carrying his food and even washing his feet.

Craig Meehan continues to live in West Yorkshire but away from the Dewsbury Moor estate. He has found it hard to find work and now prefers not to discuss the past.

He no longer receives police protection and is attempting to slip back into anonymity.

He was thought to be back in contact with Karen while she was on remand and had to be persuaded by the police not to attend her trial for fear of angering locals. It was even reported that he had proposed to Karen by letter. But the pair no longer communicate and he is believed to have a new partner who he intends to marry.

Craig's family are still in contact with him and prefer not to discuss the case. Alice Meehan claimed the stress of the trial almost drove her to suicide, coming so soon after losing her husband. She remains furious at Karen's allegations against her. 'Matthews would have done anything to save her skin,' she said.

And Caroline Meehan – who was also at one point under arrest – remains outraged at the stories Karen and Donovan told officers. Asked about her feelings towards Karen and Donovan, she said, 'They should get life.'

Karen now spends her days in prison smoking and eating. Her weight has tipped the 16-stone mark. For a spell she worked as a cleaner on her wing at New Hall Prison – for which she earned £10 a week to spend on cigarettes and chocolate. But she angered other inmates by being kept on the segregation unit for her own safety. They felt conditions in the unit were 'cushy', with inmates allowed their own kettles and televisions in their more roomy cells.

Her cleaning job also allowed Karen to get more food than other inmates as she was able to eat leftovers in the prison kitchens. Hostility towards Karen at New Hall became so great that a couple of months into her sentence she was transferred to Peterborough Jail where it was hoped she might integrate better, being further from West Yorkshire where her notoriety was greatest.

It was while she was at Peterborough, in May 2009, that Karen gave an interview to the *Daily Mirror* in which she continued to paint herself as the innocent victim in the whole saga of her daughter's abduction. 'I always get the blame for everything,' she moaned to the reporter.

And the closest thing to an apology? 'I am sorry. Sorry that I am in here serving time for something I didn't do. But I have to decide how I always go for the wrong men.' It was unclear whether she was referring to Craig or Michael – or maybe both.

She went on, 'Donovan was part of the plot to frame me. They wanted me to get the blame. It was all planned.' Referring to the 'they' that she was talking about, she said, 'I can't prove who they were but there were people whispering around me when Shannon was missing and, when I asked them what it was about, I was told nowt.'

She claimed she wanted nothing more to do with Craig but, despite her disappointments with men, she did reveal she had managed to land herself a new man while in prison – a 49-year-old former boyfriend of her sister who had started writing to her and even sent her a pair of diamond earrings.

She appeared happy in jail, with her own cell and use of a shared lounge with a pool table and widescreen TV. She also earned herself a little pocket money by serving breakfasts. As for what she missed from the outside world: 'Sex, shopping and coffee at my neighbour's house.' There was no mention of any of her seven children.

Soon after the interview, Karen ran into problems with other inmates again and she was transferred once more, this time to Bronzefied Prison in Ashfield, Middlesex – Britain's top-security prison for women, built in 2004. She receives few visitors, having broken relations with most of her friends and family. Her days are spent watching television and chatting to other inmates. No one knows how much time – if any – she dedicates to thinking about her children and how things have turned out in her life.

Although this is Shannon's story – a little girl betrayed from birth – it is also inevitably the story of Karen Matthews and why she treated her daughter the way she did. Before, during and after her trial, Karen painted herself as a victim, not just in Shannon's disappearance but in life generally. She complained her childhood was unhappy and her relationships doomed. 'They all left me,' she said when asked in court about the fathers of her children.

Not one of the dads of her kids had ever thought to marry her and she appeared so lacking in self-esteem and aspiration that she had allowed herself to be buffeted along by relationships that came and went. But, despite her difficulties, what would drive Karen to do what she did? To lie and lie and lie again, all while facing the prospect that exposure would mean losing her daughter – and most likely all her children – forever.

Reading and rereading the evidence, talking to those who know Karen and witnesses from the time, it seems most likely that Karen agreed to move in with Michael Donovan while drinking at Brian Meehan's wake.

Karen, always vulnerable and desperate for male attention, had just rowed with Craig and was depressed at the way he had been treating her. It seems he had been bullying her mentally and it was also indicated during his trial that he watched porn on his computer in front of her.

Maybe Karen and Michael had a brief fumble that night; certainly Karen was no stranger to sexual liaisons at the most inappropriate times with the most inappropriate people. Or maybe Michael simply hoped for a relationship once Karen and her kids moved in with him. She was clearly just looking for an escape route from the increasingly controlling Craig.

Maybe over the subsequent weeks she worked out the plan in her mind, convincing herself it could work. But here the motive becomes even more murky. Did Karen switch her scheme to one in which she would use Michael to take Shannon from school as agreed then report her missing and sit back and wait for the £50,000 reward to mount up? And were other people involved in the scheme from the start? Few people other than Karen Matthews know the truth – and she isn't saying.

Since Shannon first disappeared, Karen Matthews has offered five different versions of her role in the drama – none of which appears wholly convincing. First, she was the distraught mother desperate for news of her daughter's whereabouts. Second came the story on the evening she confessed when she claimed she asked Michael to look after Shannon just while she attempted to leave Craig. Third, she claimed the whole plot was Craig and his family's idea. Fourth, she again laid blame with the Meehans but alleged that they had made her take the blame for the abduction. And fifth, she again claimed she knew nothing at all about the plot and was entirely innocent.

Julie Bushby, who spent long days and nights with Karen during and after Shannon's disappearance, remained baffled as to which of these explanations lies closest to the truth. 'I personally don't think it was for the reward,' she said. 'I don't know what it was for, it could have been attention.'

And, despite his forthright denunciations immediately following the conclusion of the trial, Det Supt Brennan has revealed he too is uncertain about the whole story behind Shannon's disappearance. 'Although she [Karen] has started to give away elements of the truth,' he said, 'even now I don't think we have got the full truth from her. I don't think she will ever tell anyone the whole truth because of the seriousness of what happened.'

Possibly that full truth will never now emerge.

Whatever Karen's motive before Shannon was abducted, there is little doubt that she quickly came to enjoy her television and press appearances. She made seven television appeals in total, each carried out with incredible acting skills. Amanda Hyett may well have been right when she said Karen wanted to become the 'Kerry Katona of Dewsbury' – the ultimate dysfunctional reality star.

The television appeals gave Karen her own taste of reality TV. Tellingly, she far preferred watching rolling news coverage of the hunt for her daughter than actually getting involved in the hard work of searching for Shannon. The television appearances might have brought fame and (she hoped) fortune. But they also enabled her to be in make-believe what she had never been in real life – a devoted, loving mother who put the needs of her child first.

The Social Services psychological report completed on Karen long before Shannon's disappearance recorded that she 'always put her own needs above those of her children'. Throughout the events that followed, that was found to be totally accurate assessment.

The idea of abducting Shannon put Karen's need to flee Craig or to land herself £50,000 above the welfare of her daughter. And the refusal to answer detectives or the court honestly again put Karen's needs to claim innocence above her children's right to know the truth. In court, she retained the image of a sulky teenager being picked on by those in authority for something that 'wasn't my fault'. Nothing, according to Karen Matthews, was ever her fault: the failed relationships, the neglected children or the abduction of Shannon.

In her mind, she was a permanent victim, someone who things just happened to, like a sponge soaking up life's misfortunes: men came and left her life as they chose, children were born to her without her having any means of supporting them, brothers and sisters 'betrayed' her for no reason she could fathom.

Like a guest on her favourite daytime *Jeremy Kyle Show*, she portrayed herself throughout as the victim, the misunderstood child, the abandoned girlfriend, the wronged mother. Maybe that was why she played the role of distraught parent so well in the TV appeals; she simply delved into the well of self-pity within her.

Even now she appears to show no remorse, refusing to accept she has done anything wrong, even though in April 2009 she abandoned her plans to appeal against her conviction. By the time Karen leaves jail, Shannon will be 13. It is unknown whether they will have contact then – or whether Shannon will even want to see her mother again.

Getting caught up with trying to get inside the mind of Karen Matthews, it is all too easy to forget about the real victim – Shannon. Throughout Shannon's life, she had been overlooked because of the dramas and self-interest of her mother. And even this book risks doing the same.

But we must not forget the very real fear Shannon felt that day she was found at Lidgate Gardens, or overlook the trauma and flashbacks she suffered as a result of her ordeal. It can only be hoped that her experience will not cause too much lasting damage. Perhaps now we simply have to be content that Shannon is alive – and safe. Since her ordeal she has been reunited with her father, Leon Rose, and her siblings and is being looked after in care.

Most likely we would no longer even recognise Shannon, who turned 11 in 2009. Physically she will have changed and emotionally, away from her mother, she will hopefully have been able to develop and emerge from her 'timid' nature.

For in many ways Shannon had been missing to the people who should have been caring for her since the day she was born. Karen Matthews had always been too caught up with herself to even notice her quiet daughter.

So in the end it took her disappearance for Shannon to be truly found – found by people who will now bring her up within an atmosphere of love where she will finally be properly noticed for who she really is.